IMMIGRATION ENFORCEMENT AND POLICIES

IMMIGRATION ENFORCEMENT AND POLICIES

BRUNO T. ISENBURG
EDITOR

Nova Science Publishers, Inc.
New York

For permission to use material from this book please contact us:
Telephone 631-231-7269; Fax 631-231-8175
Web Site: http://www.novapublishers.com

Library of Congress Cataloging-in-Publication Data

Immigration enforcement and policies / Bruno T. Isenburg (editor).
p. cm.
Includes index.
ISBN 1-60021-303-0
ISBN 13: 978-1-60021-303-8
1. United States--Emigration and immigration--Government policy. 2. Emigration and immigration law--United States. 3. Illegal aliens--United States. I. Isenburg, Bruno T.
JV6483.I5543 2006
325.73--dc22 2006018936

Published by Nova Science Publishers, Inc. ✣New York

CONTENTS

PREFACE

An estimated 11 million unauthorized aliens reside in the United States, and this population is expected to increase by 500,000 annually. Each year approximately 1 million aliens are apprehended trying to enter the United States illegally. Although most of these aliens enter the United States for economic opportunities and family reunification, or to avoid civil strife and political unrest, some are criminals, and some may be terrorists. All are violating the United States' immigration laws.

In: Immigration Enforcement and Policies
Editor: B. T. Isenburg, pp. 1-94
ISBN: 1-60021-303-0

Chapter 1

IMMIGRATION ENFORCEMENT WITHIN THE UNITED STATES*

Alison Siskin, Andorra Bruno, Blas Nunez-Neto, Lisa M. Seghetti and Ruth Ellen Wasem

ABSTRACT

An estimated 11 million unauthorized aliens reside in the United States, and this population is estimated to increase by 500,000 annually. Each year, approximately 1 million aliens are apprehended trying to enter the United States illegally. Although most of these aliens enter the United States for economic opportunities and family reunification, or to avoid civil strife and political unrest, some are criminals, and some may be terrorists. All are violating the United States' immigration laws.

Immigration enforcement is the regulation of those who violate provisions of the Immigration and Nationality Act (INA). This includes violations of the INA's civil provisions (e.g., violate the conditions of their admittance), as well as U.S. citizens or aliens who violate the criminal provisions (e.g., marriage fraud or alien smuggling). Many divergent tasks are incorporated under the banner of immigration enforcement. These include removing aliens who should not be in the United States, investigating alien smuggling and trafficking, patrolling between and at ports of entry, combating document and benefit fraud, and enforcing the prohibitions against employers hiring aliens without work authorization.

---

* Excerpted from CRS Report RL33351, dated April 6, 2006.

Historically, more resources (measured in staff hours) have been allotted to enforcement at the border than enforcement within the United States. While the amount of U.S. Border Patrol (USBP) resources almost doubled between FY1997 and FY2003, time spent on other enforcement activities increased only slightly, while the number of inspection hours decreased. Furthermore, focusing on "interior" enforcement, in FY2003, the largest amount of staff time was devoted to locating and arresting criminal aliens (39%), followed by administrative and non-investigative duties (23%) and alien smuggling investigations (15%). Only 4% was devoted to worksite enforcement (i.e., locating and arresting aliens working without authorization, and punishing employers who hire such workers).

The 109th Congress has spent much time debating immigration enforcement and the unauthorized alien population. Congress could allocate more resources to immigration enforcement activities, raising the question of what is the most efficient allocation of resources among the different enforcement tasks. For example, some assert that the United States has not truly tried immigration enforcement, arguing that most of the resources have been devoted to border enforcement, instead of fully engaging in other types of immigration enforcement; others contend that only a legalization program can reduce the unauthorized population. In addition, Congress could expand the immigration enforcement role of other federal agencies and state and local law enforcement. Many fear, however, that this option will distract the agencies and local law enforcement from their primary missions. Since many of the unauthorized aliens come to the United States for economic opportunities, some argue that a guest worker program, creating opportunities for a large number of aliens to come to the United States to work, could significantly reduce unauthorized migration. Others argue that an increase in the enforcement of the prohibition against hiring illegal alien workers and the use and manufacturing of fraudulent documents would make it more difficult for unauthorized aliens to find work, resulting in a decrease in the unauthorized population. This report will not be updated.

Key Policy Staff: Immigration Enforcement

Subject Area	Analyst	Phone	E-mail
Coordinator	Alison Siskin	7-0260	asiskin@crs.loc.gov
Alien smuggling and trafficking	Alison Siskin	7-0260	asiskin@crs.loc.gov
Benefit and document fraud	Ruth Ellen Wasem	7-7342	rwasem@crs.loc.gov
Border patrol	Blas Nuñez-Neto	7-0622	bnunezneto@crs.loc.gov
Detention and removal	Alison Siskin	7-0260	asiskin@crs.loc.gov
Inspections	Blas Nuñez-Neto	7-0622	bnunezneto@crs.loc.gov
Worksite enforcement	Andorra Bruno	7-7865	abruno@crs.loc.gov

INTRODUCTION

It is estimated that there are more than 11 million unauthorized aliens[1] currently living in the United States, and the resident unauthorized alien population is estimated to increase by 500,000 people per year.[2] In addition, each year approximately 1 million aliens are apprehended while trying to illegally enter the United States. Although most of these aliens are entering the United States for economic opportunities or fleeing civil strife and political unrest, some are criminals, and some may be terrorists.[3] All are violating the immigration laws of the United States.

The existence of a large unauthorized population creates an illicit industry devoted to creating fraudulent identities and documents to aid unauthorized aliens in living and working in the United States. Illegal identity documents may be used by terrorists and other criminals who desire to remain hidden from law enforcement.[4] In addition, some argue that it would be harder for unauthorized aliens, including criminals and terrorists, to stay in the United States if finding a job were more difficult.[5] The Center for Immigration Studies found that eight of the 48 *al Qaeda* foreign born terrorists operating in the United States since 1993 worked in the United States illegally.[6]

Some have argued that the U.S. government has been unsuccessful in controlling illegal immigration due to a conflict in political will; the desire to prevent the illegal entry of those who might seek to harm the United States and its populace (e.g., terrorists, criminals), and the need to provide workers for labor-intensive industries (e.g., agriculture, food processing, restaurants). There is evidence of this conflict as far back as the mid-1800s with the arrival of Irish immigrants.[7]

Policy Issues

The large unauthorized alien population raises concerns since it is very difficult to know if any unauthorized aliens are terrorists or criminals. In addition, the existence of a underground population leads to the propagation of an illegal document industry. Nonetheless, the majority of unauthorized aliens work in the United States, raising concerns that their removal will harm the U.S. economy and illustrating a desire or need of some employers for this pool of labor. What are the best methods to decrease the unauthorized population without disrupting sectors of the economy that depend on foreign labor? Should the United States increase its efforts to reduce the unauthorized alien population, and what are the best methods and use of resources to achieve this goal? Are the current laws adequate? Should other federal agencies or local law enforcement agencies become more involved in immigration enforcement? Is the Department of Homeland Security conducting immigration enforcement in an efficient manner?

Report Overview

This report provides an analysis of immigration enforcement within the United States. The report opens with a definition of immigration enforcement, a discussion of the statutory authority to conduct immigration enforcement, and an overview of immigration enforcement related legislation since 1986. It follows with an exposition on the dichotomy of interior and border enforcement. The report then details different aspects of immigration enforcement in the United States including detention and removal, alien smuggling and trafficking, document and benefit fraud, worksite enforcement, inspections at ports of entry, and patrolling the border between ports of entry.[8] The report continues with a discussion of the role of state and local law enforcement in the enforcement of immigration laws. The report then presents a comparative analysis of the resources devoted to divergent immigration enforcement activities. It concludes with a discussion of crosscutting immigration enforcement issues related to the structure of the Department of Homeland Security. A list of acronyms is provided in the appendix.

Data and Analysis

The report uses different workload measures for the distinct immigration enforcement activities, and these measures are presented for the most current years that the data are available. For example, for the removal of aliens, the workload measure used is the number of removals, while the workload for worksite enforcement in measured in the issuance of Notices of Intent to Fine (NIF's). Nonetheless, none of these measures are comparable with each other. For example, comparing the number of NIF's issued with the number of removals does not provide any insight into the disparate resource allocation for these two tasks. In addition, due to the changes in immigration enforcement priorities after the attacks of September 11, 2001, wherever possible, measures of enforcement activities are presented prior to and after FY2001.

To compare the resources devoted to different enforcement activities, the report analyzes data on agent work hours for each enforcement activity. The data are from the Department of Homeland Security's Performance Analysis System

(PAS). The hours are presented as workyears, as 2,080 hours equal one workyear. Due to data limitations, the analysis of the hours is limited to FY1992 through FY2003. During 2004, Immigration and Customs Enforcement (ICE) and Customs and Border Protection (CBP) switched their accounting system from PAS to the U.S. Customs Service's Treasury Enforcement Communications System (TECS), and as a result, data for 2004 onward are not comparable with previous years. TECS contains fewer data fields than PAS, which means that some of the measures in PAS do not exist in TECS. In addition, the data for FY2004 are incomplete in both systems, as the different components in DHS did not switch from PAS to TECS at the same time.

WHAT IS IMMIGRATION ENFORCEMENT?

Immigration enforcement is the regulation of those who violate provisions of the Immigration and Nationality Act (INA). This includes violations of the civil provisions of the INA (e.g., aliens who enter without inspection or violate the conditions of their admittance),[9] as well as U.S. citizens or aliens who violate the criminal provisions of the INA (e.g., marriage fraud or alien smuggling).

Some of the duties under immigration law have aspects of immigration enforcement but also contain adjudicative functions (sometimes referred to as services) and are not universally considered enforcement. Immigration inspectors are the classic example of this "dual" role, as inspectors are responsible for keeping those who seek to harm U.S. interests out while letting bona fide travelers in. An alien who is denied entry to the United States by an inspector has not violated any provision of the INA, unless the alien has committed some type of fraud to gain entry. Indeed, there have been people (both aliens and U.S. citizens) who have been wrongly denied entry by an immigration inspector. It could also be argued that a Department of Homeland Security (DHS) Citizenship and Immigration Services (USCIS) adjudicator is performing an enforcement function by denying an alien's application for a benefit to which he is not entitled. Others would argue that this is an example of a purely adjudicative function, for unless the alien has committed fraud to receive the benefit, he or she has not committed a violation under the INA.

According to DHS, immigration enforcement should be viewed as part of a comprehensive homeland security strategy that unifies and coordinates law enforcement operations across formerly separate agencies (e.g., the Immigration and Naturalization Service (INS), the Federal Protective Service, the U.S. Coast Guard, and the U.S. Customs Service).[10] The former Commissioner of INS,[11]

James Zigler, was quoted as saying, "We need to set up a regime where we don't have to spend so much of our time and effort in enforcement activities dealing with people who are not terrorists, who are not threats to our national security, who are economic refugees."[12]

Some argue that since the terrorists responsible for the 9/11 attacks were aliens, immigration enforcement has recently had an anti-terrorism focus. Moreover, the Center for Immigration Studies found that at least 22 of the 48 al Qaeda foreign-born terrorists found operating in the United States since 1993 had committed significant violations of immigration laws[13] Thus, it can be argued that more stringent enforcement of the immigration laws may have disrupted some of the terrorists' plans.

Authority to Conduct Immigration Enforcement[14]

The Immigration and Nationality Act (INA), as amended, is the primary law by which Congress legislates on immigration.[15] Basic enforcement authority for immigration officials stems from §287 and §235 of the INA.[16] INA §287 gives any officer or employee of the former INS (now employees of the DHS) authorized under regulation prescribed by the Attorney General (now the Secretary of DHS) the general power, without a warrant, to interrogate aliens, make arrests, conduct searches, board vessels, and administer oaths.[17] INA §235 authorizes "immigration officers" to inspect all aliens who are applicants for admission or otherwise seeking admission or readmission to or transit through the United States. As evidenced above, the INA makes no distinction in its law enforcement provisions between the various types of employees or officers of the former INS (e.g., border patrol (USBP), investigators, and deportation officers). Rather, it is through regulation where specific types of DHS personnel, including the USBP, are authorized and designated to conduct certain law enforcement activities.[18]

Overview of Select Major Immigration Enforcement Legislation Since 1986

Since 1986, there have been several bills with major immigration enforcement provisions. The following highlights some of the most important enacted legislation for immigration enforcement activities in the United States, and provides a brief summary of the important changes. The enacted immigration enforcement legislation includes the:

- Immigration Reform and Control Act of 1986 (IRCA; P.L. 99-603), which addressed the control of illegal immigration by creating sanctions for employers who hire or continue to employ aliens who are not authorized to work, and by legalizing most of the unauthorized aliens present in the United States at that time;
- Violent Crime Control and Law Enforcement Act of 1994 (P.L. 103-322), which gave the Attorney General the option to bypass deportation proceedings for certain alien aggravated felons, enhanced penalties for alien smuggling and reentry after deportation, and increased appropriations for the border patrol;
- Illegal Immigration Reform and Immigrant Responsibility Act of 1996 (IIRIRA; P.L. 104-208), which added to the grounds of inadmissibility and deportability, expanded the list of crimes constituting an aggravated felony, created expedited removal procedures, and reduced the judicial review of immigration decisions;
- USA Patriot Act of 2001 (P.L. 107-56), which broadened the terrorism grounds for excluding aliens from entering the United States, and increased monitoring of foreign students;
- Enhanced Border Control and Visa Reform Act of 2002 (P.L. 107-173), which required the development of an interoperable electronic data system to be used to share information relevant to alien admissibility and removability, and required the implementation of an integrated entry-exit data system;[19]
- Homeland Security Act of 2002 (P.L. 107-296), which transferred the majority of INS' functions to DHS, leaving the Executive Office of Immigration Review in the Department of Justice;[20]
- National Intelligence Reform Act of 2004 (P.L. 108-458), which expanded the grounds of inadmissibility and deportability, accelerated the deployment of the entry/exit system, and increased criminal penalties for alien smuggling;[21] and
- REAL ID Act of 2005 (P.L. 109-13), which established statutory guidelines for removal cases, expanded the terrorism-related grounds for inadmissibility and deportation, included measures to improve border infrastructure, and required states to verify an applicant's legal status before issuing a driver's license or personal identification card that may be accepted for any federal purpose.[22]

Interior vs. Border

Although many make the distinction between interior and border enforcement, questions have been raised about the usefulness of the distinction. Many immigration professionals do not accept the rationale that there is a distinct interior enforcement mission, since interior enforcement can be viewed as a continuum of border enforcement (i.e., violators not caught at the border, must be apprehended and processed in the interior).[23] However, certain aspects of interior enforcement lack a border component. For example, fugitive taskforces, investigations of alien slavery and sweatshops, and employer sanctions do not require close coordination between DHS Customs and Border Protection (CBP) and DHS Immigration and Customs Enforcement (ICE). As an illustration that not all enforcement activities contain a border component, in FY2004, CBP referrals accounted for only 23% of all ICE criminal investigations.[24]

Interior Enforcement Strategies

A Government Accountability Study (GAO) report in October 2004 found that although ICE does not have a formal interior enforcement strategy, all the objectives contained in INS interior enforcement strategy have been incorporated within a broader mission to strengthen homeland security.[25] INS interior enforcement strategy, issued in 1999, was designed to address, in order of priority, (1) the detention and removal of criminal aliens, (2) the dismantling and diminishing of alien smuggling and trafficking operations, (3) community complaints about illegal immigration including those of law enforcement, (4) immigrant benefit and document fraud, and (5) employers' use of unauthorized aliens. Overall, the strategy aimed to deter illegal immigration, prevent immigration related crimes, and remove those illegally in the United States.

Two ICE offices, the Office of Investigations (OI) and the Office of Detention and Removal (DRO), bear the primary responsibility for immigration interior enforcement functions.[26] OI is responsible for addressing smuggling and trafficking in aliens, benefit fraud, responding to community complaints of illegal immigrations, and worksite enforcement.[27] DRO is responsible for identifying and removing criminal aliens with some assistance from OI.[28] In addition, the compliance unit within ICE's National Security Investigations Division analyzes data from various databases, such as United States Visitor and Immigrant Status Indicator Technology (US-VISIT) Program and the Student and Exchange Visitor Information System (SEVIS), to identify those who may have violated the terms of their entry or be a risk to national security.

Border Enforcement

Border enforcement includes inspections at ports of entry (POEs) and the patrolling of areas between POEs.[29] In 1994, the USBP strategy to deter illegal entry was "prevention through deterrence," i.e., to raise the risk of being apprehended to the point where aliens would find it futile to try to enter. The strategy called for placing USBP resources and manpower directly at the areas of greatest illegal immigration in order to detect, deter, and apprehend aliens attempting to cross the border between official points of entry.[30]

After September 11, 2001, the USBP refocused its strategy on preventing the entry of terrorists and weapons of mass destruction. In order to prevent and deter terrorist entry, intelligence and surveillance operations have been focused on known smuggling operations that have previously trafficked aliens from significant interest countries. The USBP also coordinates and shares intelligence with Canadian and Mexican authorities. It is important to note, however, that the increased emphasis on preventing terrorist entry into the United States did not change the scope of the USBP's mission — preventing unauthorized aliens from entering the country. There is evidence that although border enforcement has increased, forcing aliens to take more dangerous routes to enter the United States, and increasing the risks and costs of those attempting to illegally enter the United States, the number of unauthorized aliens in the United States has continued to increase.[31]

TYPES OF IMMIGRATION ENFORCEMENT

The INA includes both criminal and civil components, providing both for criminal charges (e.g., alien smuggling, which is prosecuted in the federal courts) and for civil violations (e.g., lack of legal status, which may lead to removal through a separate administrative system in the Department of Justice).[32] Being illegally present in the U.S. has always been a civil, not criminal, violation of the INA, and subsequent deportation and associated administrative processes are civil proceedings.[33] For instance, a lawfully admitted nonimmigrant alien may become deportable if his visitor's visa expires or if his student status changes. Criminal violations of the INA, on the other hand, include felonies and misdemeanors and are prosecuted in federal district courts. These types of violations include the bringing in and harboring of certain undocumented aliens (INA §274), the illegal entry of aliens (INA §275), and the reentry of aliens previously excluded or deported (INA §276).[34]

Removal (Deportation)

An alien is "removable" if (1) the alien has not been admitted to the United States and is inadmissible under INA §212,[35] or (2) the alien has been admitted to the United States and is deportable under INA §237. The Illegal Immigration Reform and Immigrant Responsibility Act of 1996 (IIRIRA) combined "exclusion" and "deportation" proceedings into a single removal proceeding. INA §237 specifies six broad classes of deportable aliens including aliens who:

- are inadmissible at time of entry or violate their immigration status;[36]
- commit certain criminal offenses (e.g., crimes of moral turpitude,[37] aggravated felonies,[38] alien smuggling, high speed flight);
- fail to register (if required under law) or commit document fraud;
- are security risks (such as aliens who violate any law relating to espionage, engage in criminal activity which endangers public safety, partake in terrorist activities, or assisted in Nazi persecution or genocide);
- become a public charge within five years of entry;[39] or
- vote unlawfully.

In removal proceedings an immigration judge (IJ) from the Department of Justice's Executive Office for Immigration Review (EOIR) determines whether an alien is removable. The proceeding commences when the alien is issued a notice to appear (NTA) which can be issued by a variety of DHS personnel including border patrol officers in CBP, asylum and examination officers in USCIS, and detention officers in ICE.[40]

With certain exceptions, a removal proceeding under INA §240 is the "exclusive procedure" for determining whether an alien should be removed from the United States. These exceptions include expedited removal (INA §235, and removal proceedings under the Institutional Removal Program (IRP). Those who are removed are subject to bars to reenter the country.[41]

The courts have ruled that removal proceedings are civil not criminal, and that deportation is not punishment. Thus, there is no right to counsel, no right to a jury trial, and the due process protections are less than in a criminal trial. Furthermore, a decision on removablity does not have to be proven beyond a reasonable doubt. In addition, because deportation is not punishment, Congress may impose new immigration consequences for actions that previously occurred (i.e., actions that would not have made the alien deportable when they occurred may make the alien deportable at a later date if Congress changes the law).[42]

Expedited Removal[43]

Under expedited removal, an alien who lacks proper documentation or has committed fraud or willful misrepresentation of facts to gain admission into the United States is inadmissible and may be removed from the United States without any further hearings or review,[44] unless the alien indicates either an intention to apply for asylum or a fear of persecution.[45]

Aliens subject to expedited removal must be detained until they are removed and may only be released due to medical emergency or if necessary for law enforcement purposes. Although under law the Attorney General[46] may apply expedited removal to any alien who has not been admitted or paroled[47] into the United States and cannot show that they have been continuously present for two years, expedited removal has only been applied to aliens

- arriving at ports of entry;
- arriving by sea who are not admitted or paroled; and, recently,
- who are present without being admitted or paroled, are encountered by an immigration officer within 100 air miles of the U.S. international land border, and have not established to the satisfaction of an immigration officer that they have been physically present in the United States continuously for the 14-day period immediately preceding the date of encounter.

Institutional Removal Program

INA §238(a) allows for removal proceedings to be conducted at federal, state, and local prisons for aliens convicted of crimes. This program as instituted is known as the Institutional Removal Program (IRP). Under the IRP, the proceedings are held while the alien is incarcerated. Nonetheless, under the INA aliens must complete their criminal sentences before they can be removed from the United States.[48] INS developed a nationwide automated tracking system for the federal Bureau of Prisons (BOP) and deployed them to IRP sites. The system covers foreign born inmates incarcerated under the federal system and tracks the hearing status of each inmate.[49]

Removal Proceedings

As discussed above, when DHS encounters an alien that it thinks should be removed from the United States, the alien is presented a notice to appear (NTA), which commences the removal proceeding. The NTA outlines the charges against the alien and identifies the part of the INA that the alien is being charged with violating. If the alien is not subject to mandatory detention (discussed below), the alien may be detained, or released on bond or his own recognizance (OR).[50]

In a court removal proceeding an ICE attorney (i.e., the government's attorney) must prove the charges in the NTA, witnesses are presented, and the immigration judge rules on whether the alien is removable from the United States or is eligible for relief from removal.[51] An alien who fails to appear for a removal hearing (absent exceptional circumstances) can be removed in absentia and becomes inadmissible for five years,[52] and ineligible for relief from removal for 10 years.[53] Within 30 days after the hearing, the government's attorney or the alien may appeal the decision to the Board of Immigration Appeals (BIA) in EOIR. After the BIA decision the alien may appeal to a federal court.

Voluntary Departure

The majority of aliens who are removed do not undergo formal removal proceedings in front of an IJ. Most aliens are given the opportunity to depart voluntarily from the United States, and most of them agree to voluntary departure.[54] At the border, voluntary departure is only available for aliens from contiguous territories (i.e., Canada and Mexico), and aliens are escorted to the point of departure.[55] CBP inspectors also can permit an alien traveling through a POE to withdraw their application for admission and return to their point of origin. Aliens who do not take one of these options (and are not under expedited removal), when offered, are subject to formal removal proceedings in front of a DOJ immigration judge and ICE's Office of Detention and Removal (DRO) assumes responsibility for the alien's custody management (detention or release, and possible reapprehension of released aliens) and removal of the alien (which may include escorting the alien to their home country).[56]

In addition, certain aliens who have been issued NTA's may request voluntary departure before (in lieu of), during or after formal removal proceedings. Criminal aliens are ineligible for voluntary departure. The DHS officer or the IJ must specify the period of time allowed for departure[57] and may impose conditions, such as bond or detention, deemed necessary to assure the alien's departure.[58] Voluntary departure is not available to any alien who was previously allowed to depart voluntarily. Furthermore, aliens who fail to depart within the time period specified for voluntary departure are subject to monetary penalties and ineligible for voluntary departure or other relief from removal for 10 years.

Voluntary departure costs less than formal removal since, in most cases, the government does not have to pay for the alien's repatriation. In addition, the resources that would be needed if all aliens apprehended along the borders were subject to formal removal proceedings would be prohibitive. Nonetheless, in the interior, many aliens subject to voluntary departure fail to leave the country. It is estimated that each year, 40,000 non-detained aliens fail to leave the United States as ordered (either under voluntary departure or as ordered by an IJ).[59]

Absconder Initiative

Designed by the Office of Detention and Removal (DRO) in January 2002, and run by both DRO and OI, the National Fugitive Operations Program (NFOP) seeks to apprehend, process, and remove aliens who have failed to comply with removal orders. As part of the Alien Absconder Initiative, NFOP teams work exclusively on fugitive cases, giving priority to aliens convicted of crimes.[60] The absconder initiative was the first systematic attempt to enforce every final removal order issued.[61] Nonetheless, as Figure 1 shows, although there has been a concerted effort since FY2002 to remove absconders, the number of absconders went from 376,003 in FY2002 to 536,644 in FY2005, an increase of 43% in three years. However, this increase could be due to the increase in aliens who are given final orders of removal. In FY2001, 282,396 aliens received final orders of removal, while in FY2005, 368,848 final orders were issued.[62]

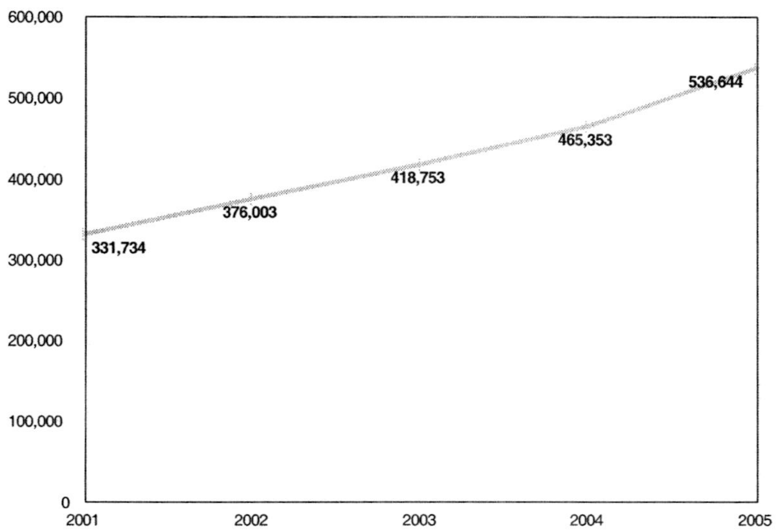

Source: CRS presentation of unpublished data from the Department of Homeland Securtity.

Figure 1. Number of Alien Absconders, FY2000-FY2005.

Criminal Aliens

Criminal aliens are aliens who have committed crimes that make them removable. The potential pool of removable criminal aliens is in the hundreds of thousands. Some are incarcerated in federal, state, or local facilities, while others are free across the United States, because they have already served their criminal sentences.[63] DHS' Criminal Alien Program is directed at identifying criminal aliens in federal, state, and local prisons, and assuring that these aliens are taken into ICE custody at the completion of their criminal sentences. Although federal prisons have a system to notify ICE when there is an alien in custody, notification from state and local prisons and jails is not systematic, and many criminal aliens are released after their criminal sentences are completed rather than taken into ICE custody, making it more difficult to locate the aliens for deportation and raising the concern that the released aliens will commit new crimes. Like ICE, INS had historically failed to identify all removable imprisoned aliens.[64]

Removal Statistics

The number of removals has declined since FY2000 (See Figure 2). In FY2000, INS removed 1.9 million aliens, the largest number of aliens removed in a single year. The total number of removals declined from FY2000 to FY2003, but increased in FY2004.

The decline in total removals was due primarily to a decrease in the number of voluntary departures. As Figure 3 shows, the number of formal removals significantly increased after FY1996, when the Illegal Immigration Reform and Immigrant Responsibility Act of 1996 made more crimes deportable offenses, increasing the number of aliens required to undergo formal removal proceedings.[65] In FY1996, there were 69,680 formal removals. The number of formal removals continuously increased between FY1996 and FY2000, then decreased in FY2001 and FY2002. The decrease between FY2001 and FY2002, may have been the result of a backlog in cases before the Board of Immigration Appeals (BIA).[66] Since FY2002, the number of formal removals has increased, reaching an all-time high of 204,193 aliens in FY2005. The increase in formal removals in FY2003, could be attributed to the Attorney General's decision to streamline the immigration appeals process, see discussion below.

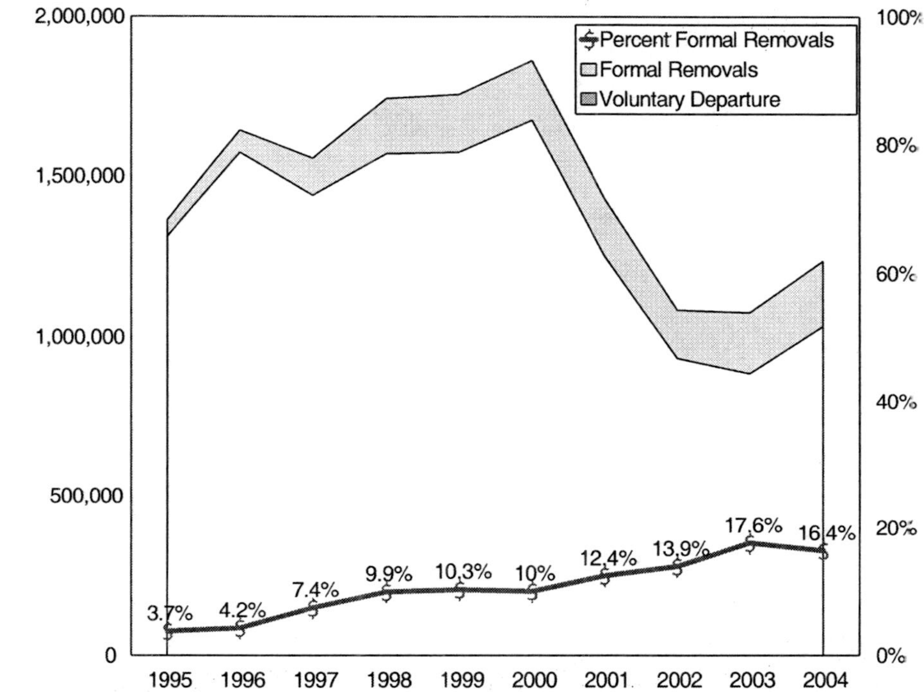

	1995	1996	1997	1998	1999	2000	2001	2002	2003	2004
Formal Removals	50,924	69,680	114,432	173,146	181,072	186,222	178,026	150,542	189,368	202,842
Voluntary Departure	1,313,764	1,573,428	1,440,684	1,570,127	1,574,682	1,675,711	1,254,035	934,119	887,115	1,035,477
Total	1,364,688	1,643,108	1,555,116	1,743,273	1,755,754	1,861,933	1,432,061	1,084,661	1,076,483	1,238,319

Source: DHS Office of Immigration Statistics, *FY2004 Yearbook of Immigration Statistics*, January 2006, p. 159.

Figure 2. Types of Removals: FY1995-FY2004.

As previously noted, most of the removals from the United States are voluntary departures as opposed to formal removals. Figure 2 illustrates the percent of formal removals compared to all removals increased steadily between FY1996 and FY2003, and then decreased in slightly between FY2003 and FY2004. The decrease was most likely the result of a decrease in apprehensions along the border (discussed below). In FY1996, 4.2% of all removals were formal removals, compared to 17.6% in FY2003. In FY2004, 16.4% of all removed aliens went through the formal removal process.

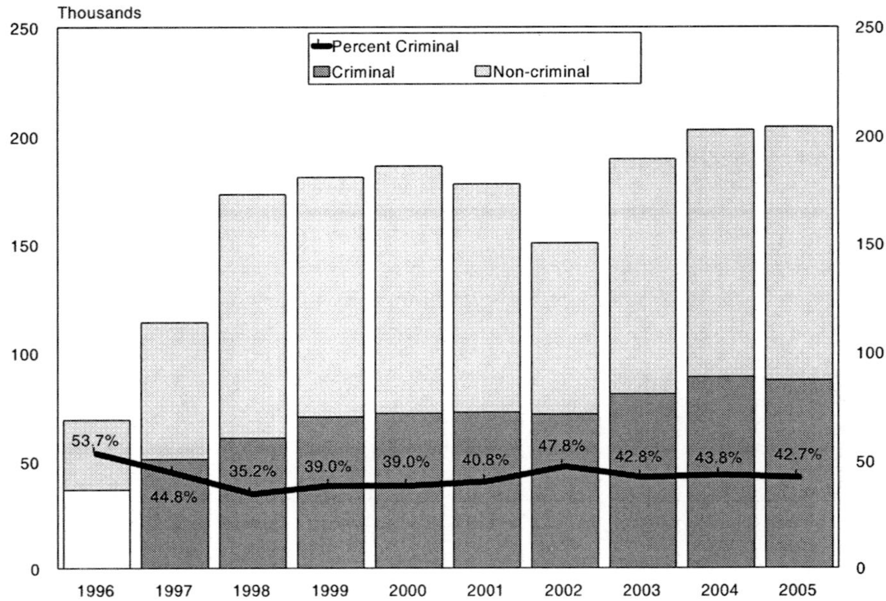

Source: FY1996-FY1997 from Immigration and Naturalization Service, *FY1997 Statistical Yearbook of the INS.* FY1998-FY2004 from DHS Office of Immigration Statistics, *FY2004 Yearbook of Immigration Statistics,* January 2006, p. 162. FY2005, DHS, *FY2005 Monthly Statistical Report, Year End,* September 2005.

Figure 3. Criminal and Noncriminal Formal Removals: FY1996-FY2005

In addition, as Figure 3 demonstrates, since FY1996, the majority of aliens formally removed were noncriminal aliens. In FY1996, 53.7% of all formal removals were criminal aliens; since then, noncriminal aliens have comprised the majority of formally removed aliens. In FY2005, 42.7% of formally removed aliens were criminal aliens.

As shown in Figure 4, the three most common reasons for formal removals are (1) attempted illegal entry; (2) criminal grounds (i.e., committing a crime in the United States); and (3) not in status (i.e., unlawful presence). In addition, the proportion of the formally removed population which was removed due to being previously removed increased almost threefold between 1995 and 2004.

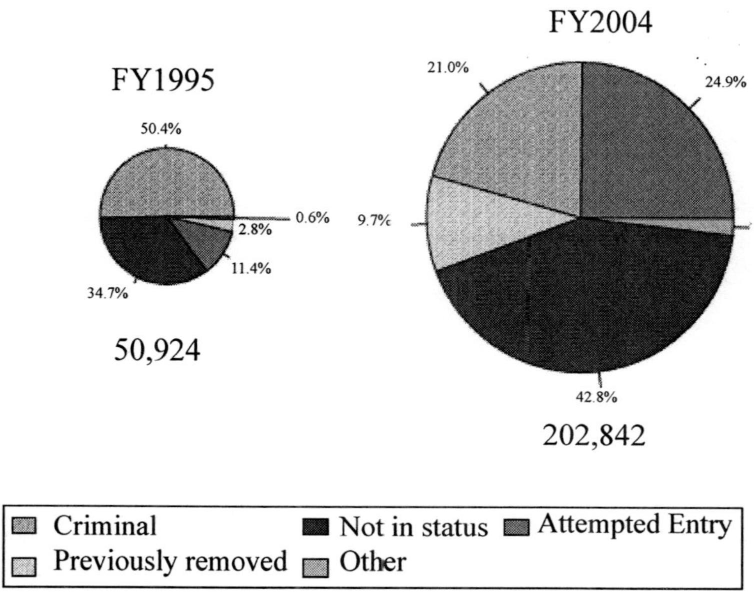

Source: DHS, Yearbook of Immigration Statistics, FY2004.

Figure 4. Formal Removal by Reason: FY1995 and FY2004.

Selected Removal Issues

The government's ability to remove aliens who do not have permission to be in the United States, or have violated the terms of their admission (e.g., aliens who commit crimes) has been an issue of continual interest for Congress. As discussed above, there are an estimated 11 million unauthorized aliens residing in the United States. Following is a discussion of some of the reasons why the removal policy has been unable to keep pace with the unauthorized population.

Number of Investigators

On June 4, 2002, the INS had 1,944 on-duty special agents including supervisors, fewer than the number of officers in the Dallas police department.[67] In any given day, there were only 1,365 special agents to investigate fraud and smuggling cases, conduct enforcement operations at work sites, support local task forces, respond to local law enforcement officials, arrest immigration violators, and assist the Federal Bureau of Investigation (FBI) in their counterterrorism work.[68] The number of agents has a direct impact on the ability of ICE to be able to remove unauthorized aliens, as ICE agents are charged with locating and arresting removable aliens. In 2002, there were an estimated 9.3

million unauthorized aliens in the United States, which was approximately 4,784 unauthorized aliens per special agent.

The number of ICE special agents increased from a total of 5,449 in FY2003 to 5,614 in FY2004, and 5,769 in FY2005.[69] However, since agents from the former INS and the former U.S. Customs Service were combined into ICE, it is unknown what percentage of time the ICE special agents spend on immigration enforcement functions compared to tasks of the former U.S. Customs Service. As a result, it is not known if and to what extent the number of agents devoted to immigration enforcement has increased since the creation of DHS.

Executive Office for Immigration Review

The ability to remove aliens is also influenced by the functioning of the immigration courts, as formally removed aliens who are not in expedited removal are entitled to a hearing before the courts. In FY2002, there was concern about the backlog of cases before the Board of Immigration Appeals (BIA).[70] As a result, then Attorney General John Ashcroft, made changes to streamline the appellate review within the immigration courts.

Recently, there has been an increase in immigration cases before the federal appeals courts. As Figure 5 shows, between FY2000 and FY2005, the number of appeals has increased sevenfold, while the number of cases heard by BIA during the same time increased 43%. Immigration cases increased from 3.2% of the federal appeals court's workload in FY2000, to 18% of the workload in FY2005. In addition, some federal appeals judges have harshly criticized the BIA and immigration judges. Some appeals judges argue that the streamlining of the BIA has shifted the work to their courts.[71] When a federal appeals judge overturns the decision of an immigration judge, the case is returned to EOIR to be heard by a different immigration judge, increasing the alien's time in removal proceedings (i.e., the length of the removal process) and increasing the use of EOIR resources. If the alien is being detained, the delay in finalizing a removal decision also increases the consumption of detention resources.

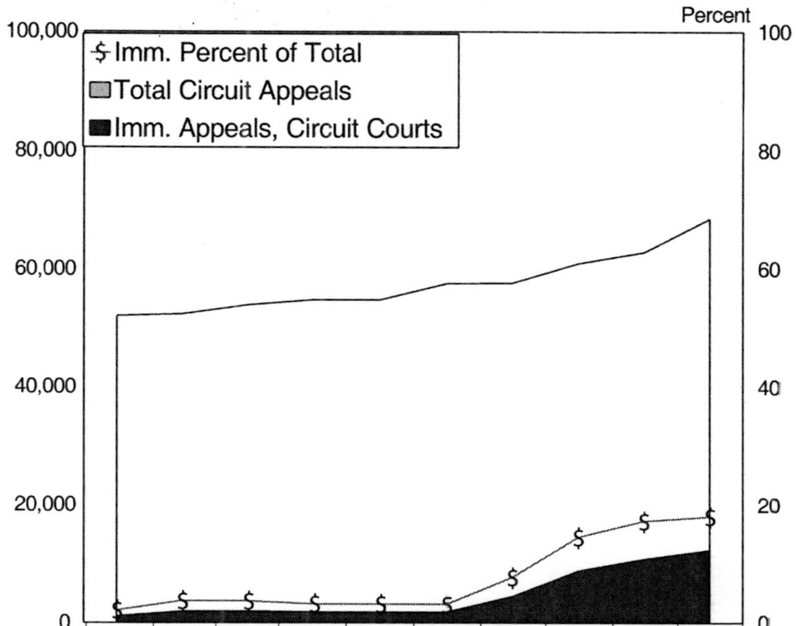

	1996	1997	1998	1999	2000	2001	2002	2003	2004	2005
Total BIA Cases	24,919	30,626	28,320	30,759	29,847	28 148	34,834	42,043	43,075	42,734
Total Circuit Appeals	51,991	52,319	53,805	54,693	54,697	57,464	57,555	60,847	62,762	68,473
Imm. Appeals, Circuit Courts	1,063	1,921	1,936	1,731	1,723	1,760	4,449	8,833	10,812	12,349

Source: Administrative Office of the U.S. Courts, *Judicial Business*, and U.S. Department of Justice, Executive Office for Immigration Review, *Statistical Yearbooks*.

Figure 5. BIA Cases, Total Appeals and Immigration Appeals before the Circuit Courts: FY1996-FY2005.

Long-Term Residents and Children

In addition, there are some policy concerns surrounding the deportation of aliens who have lived in the United States for many years and established community ties. Deportation (removal) can be controversial and seem punitive for those who have been in the United States for long periods of time and for those who entered the United States as young children and know no other country. Long term residents often have to abandon homes and businesses when they are deported. In addition, these aliens often have ties in the communities where they reside, which can result in a backlash when the government attempts to remove the alien.[72]

Furthermore, some countries (e.g., Vietnam) refuse to accept the return of their nationals who entered the United States as children. These children often have few ties to their birth countries, and may not speak the language.[73] If the alien is being deported due to a criminal act, the home countries often contend that since U.S. society created the person's antisocial behavior, the United States should take responsibility for the person. However, others note that if these aliens had not violated the laws of the United States they would not be removable.

Detention

The INA (§236) provides broad authority to detain aliens while awaiting a determination of whether they should be removed from the United States, and specifies categories of aliens subject to mandatory detention.[74] Aliens not subject to mandatory detention may be detained, paroled, or released on bond or their own recognizance. Decisions on parole made by the Secretary of DHS and bond decisions made by the Attorney General are not subject to review. Aliens paroled or released may be rearrested at any time.

The large majority of detained aliens have committed a crime while in the United States, have served their criminal sentence, and are detained while undergoing removal proceedings. Other detained aliens include those who arrive at a port of entry without proper documentation (i.e., expedited removal), but most of these aliens are quickly returned to their country of origin.[75] The majority of aliens arriving without proper documentation who claim asylum are held until their "credible fear hearing," but some of these aliens are held until their asylum claims have been adjudicated.

The Office of Detention and Removal (DRO) in ICE is responsible for the daily detention of aliens, but under law the Attorney General may still retain the authority to arrest and detain aliens. The Illegal Immigrant Reform and Immigrant Responsibility Act of 1996 (IIRIRA) amended the INA, effectively specifying levels of detention priority and classes of aliens subject to mandatory detention. Mandatory detention is required for certain criminal and terrorist aliens who are removable, pending a final decision on whether the alien is to be removed.

In October 1998, the former INS issued a memorandum establishing detention guidelines consistent with the changes made by IIRIRA.[76] According to the guidelines, detainees are assigned to one of four detention categories: (1) required, (2) high priority, (3) medium priority, and (4) lower priority.[77] Aliens in required detention are mandatory detainees,[78] while aliens in the other categories may be detained depending on detention space and the facts of the case. Higher priority aliens should be detained before aliens of lower priority.[79] Additionally, the USA-PATRIOT Act[80] amended the INA to create a new section (236A), which requires the detention of an alien whom the Attorney

General certifies as someone the Attorney General has "reasonable grounds" to believe is involved in terrorist activities or in any other activity that endangers national security.

In June 2005, 87% of detention bed space was filled with mandatory detainees, making bed space scarce and increasing the need for both good management of detention space, and alternative forms of detention.[81] A lack of bedspace can lead to an increase in the number of apprehended aliens who must be released into the community, and aliens who are not detained are less likely to appear for their removal proceedings and to leave the country if they are ordered removed. For example, in FY2005, 60% of nondetained aliens failed to appear for their removal hearing.[82] Moreover, only 18% of aliens released into the community who subsequently receive final removal orders leave the United States.[83] To counteract the high percentage of nondetained aliens who fail to leave the United States, DHS has a pilot program which began in Hartford, Connecticut, and was expanded to Atlanta and Denver in March 2004, that immediately detains all aliens subject to final orders of removal, so that ICE can ensure that the aliens depart from the United States.

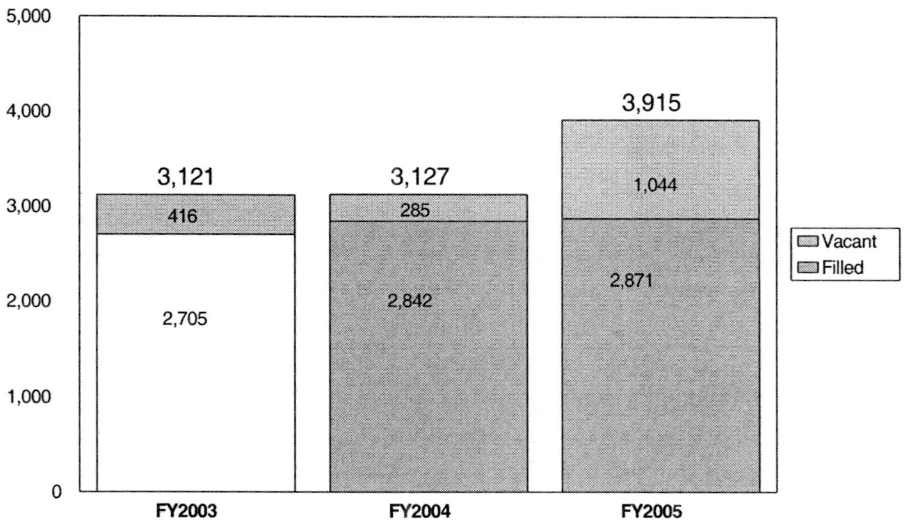

Source: CRS presentation of unpublished data from DHS.

Note: In FY2005, DRO received an additional 788 positions through budget enhancements but ICE was under a hiring freeze.

Figure 6. Number of Permanent Law Enforcement Officers in DRO, Filled and Vacant Positions: FY2003-FY2005.

Detention Statistics

Although Congress increased the number of DRO officer positions by 25% between FY2004 and FY2005, the actual number of officers increased only slightly (see Figure 6), affecting the ability of DRO to detain and remove aliens. From FY2003 to FY2004, the number of officer positions increased by only six, but the actual number of officers working increased by 139, as the number of vacancies deceased. From FY2004 to FY2005, although the total number of officers increased by 788, the number of filled positions increased slightly, from 2,842 to 2,871, while the number of vacancies increased almost threefold. The lack of actual hires was the result of financial management issues, which lead to a hiring freeze in ICE and DRO between March 2004 and May 2005.[84]

As Figure 7 shows, between FY1994 and FY2001 the average size of the daily noncitizen detention population increased steadily. There was a slight decrease in the size of the detention population between FY2001 and FY2002, and then a steady increase between FY2002 and FY2004. The daily population decreased between FY2004 and FY2005 and then increased in the beginning of FY2006. The size of the daily population increased by 129%, from 9,011 to 20,594, between FY1996, when IIRIRA was enacted, and FY2006. The largest increase occurred between FY1997 and FY1998, the year that all the provisions of the IIRIRA became enforceable. Some argue that the size of the detained population is dependent on the amount of detention space. Thus, the increase in the detained population after FY1998 reflects an increase in detention space, not in the number of people eligible to be detained.

Selected Detention Issues

Since most nondetained aliens remain illegally in the United States, the detention of noncitizens relative to the availability of bedspace has been an ongoing Congressional issue.[85] Many contend that DHS does not have enough detention space to house all those who should be detained. They contend that the increase in the number of classes of aliens subject to mandatory detention has impacted the availability of detention space for lower priority detainees. There are over half a million aliens in the United States who have been ordered deported who are presumed to still be in the country. Some argue that these aliens would have left the country if they had been detained once they were ordered deported. As discussed above, only 18% of nondetained aliens with final orders of removal leave the United States. On the other hand, 94% of detained aliens who were part of the Hartford Pilot (mentioned above) were deported. Concerns have been raised that decisions about which aliens to release and when to release them may be based on the amount of detention space, not on the merits of individual cases, and that the amount of space may vary by area of the country, leading to inequities and disparate policies in different geographic areas.[86]

Furthermore, the overall increase in the number of noncitizens in DHS detention has raised questions about the cost of detaining noncitizens. For FY2004, DHS budgeted $80 a day for each detainee held in detention.[87] This cost does not include transportation or the cost of deporting the alien.

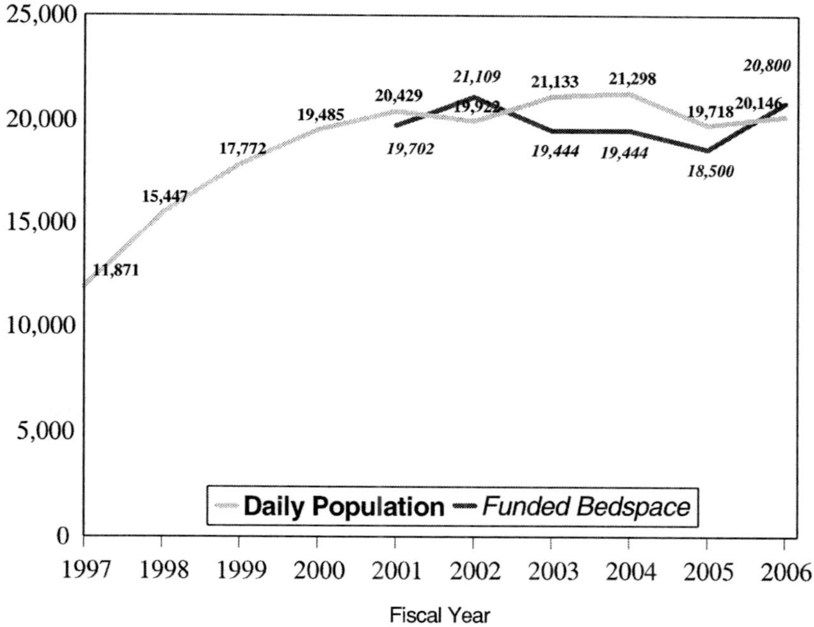

Source: FY1997 through FY2002 CRS presentation of published DHS data. FY2004 through FY2006 CRS presentation of unpublished DHS data.

Note: FY2006 is the average daily population in detention through January 30, 2006.

Figure 7. Average Daily Detention Population: FY1997-FY2006, and Funded Bedspace: FY2001-FY2006.

Figure 7 reveals that generally the daily detention population is higher than the funded number of beds. In FY2003 through FY2005, on average there were more than 1,000 aliens detained above funded bedspace, which implies that the funding to detain these aliens needs to be taken from elsewhere in DRO's or ICE's budget. In FY2006, so far the funded number of beds has outpaced the daily population.

Coordination Between CBP and ICE

Reportedly, Immigration and Customs Enforcement's (ICE's) funding and accounting difficulties, as well as the failure to coordinate planning and budgets between ICE and Customs and Border Protection (CBP) has contributed to a resource imbalance. As CBP's apprehension capabilities grew, ICE's detention and removal capabilities did not. The imbalance has placed an increasing strain on the Office of Detention and Removal (DRO) resources, as well as impacted CBP's alien apprehensions.

There is no organizational requirement that CBP notify ICE's DRO of its apprehension initiatives and expected need for detention resources. Similarly, ICE is under no obligation to notify CBP about any new initiatives which may impact the availability of detention and removal resources.[88] In addition, although at points DRO units are responsible for the transport of aliens in CBP custody, some CBP officials have said that DRO is not providing the level of transport required, and as a result, the United States Border Patrol has had to assume an increasing share of transportation responsibilities.[89] Improved coordination between the ICE and CBP may have reduced the negative impact of this resource imbalance; however, DRO's removal functions are ultimately governed by appropriations. Better coordination can improve allocation of limited resources but the agency is still constrained by the funds available for detention space and removal costs.[90]

Alien Smuggling and Trafficking

The INA specifies criminal penalties for bringing in and harboring certain aliens, commonly referred to as alien smuggling. Specifically, INA §274 prohibits and specifies penalties for any person who:

- attempts to bring in an alien at any place other than a POE;
- knowing or in reckless disregard that an alien is illegally present transports the alien within the United States;
- conceals, harbors, or shields the alien knowing or in reckless disregard that the alien is illegally present; and
- encourages or induces an alien to come to the United States, knowing or in reckless disregard that the alien will be illegally present.[91]

In addition, there are separate penalties for any person who aids or assists an alien who is inadmissible on criminal or security grounds, or brings in an alien for immoral purposes.[92]

Alien smuggling is a transnational crime due to the fact that it involves more than one country,[93] and typically the alien has consented (even paid) to be smuggled. In most cases when the aliens reach their destination, they have no continuing relationship with the smuggler.[94] In human trafficking, the alien may agree to be smuggled into the United States, but once they arrive they are subjected to exploitive arrangements, including prostitution or forced labor, that produce long-term profits for the trafficker. Under immigration law, a trafficked alien is a victim, while an alien who consents to be smuggled may be subject to criminal prosecution and deportation.

Alien smuggling and trafficking investigations are often complicated by language and humanitarian issues (e.g., the alien has been traumatized and is unable to aid in the investigation), as well as logistical challenges and difficulties (e.g., transporting, housing, and processing aliens). In addition, certain types of investigative techniques, such as controlled delivery operations,[95] cannot be used as humans are involved. Moreover, unlike drug trafficking cases where the contraband itself is proof of the illegal activity, the successful prosecution of alien smuggling cases relies on the availability of witnesses (unauthorized aliens) who may refuse to testify because of fear of retribution against themselves or their families.[96]

Many contend that alien smuggling of persons into the United States constitutes a significant risk to national security and public safety.[97] Since smugglers facilitate the illegal entry of persons into the United States, terrorists may use smuggling routes and organizations to enter undetected. It is estimated that the international alien smuggling and sex trafficking trade generates $9.5 billion for criminal organizations worldwide, and the profits are used to finance additional criminal enterprises, such as the trafficking of drugs, weapons, or other contraband.[98]

In addition to generating billions of dollars in revenues for criminal enterprises,[99] alien smuggling can lead to collateral crimes including kidnaping, homicide, assault, rape, robbery, auto theft, high speed flight, vehicle accidents, identity theft, and the manufacturing and distribution of fraudulent documents. For example, smugglers may hold an alien hostage to extort a ransom from the alien's family.[100] In addition, smugglers often establish "safe houses" (also called "drop houses") where aliens are kept until they can be moved into the interior of the United States. The often squalid conditions of these "safe houses" endanger the lives of the aliens and create health and safety issues for people living in the community.[101] Also, others note an increase in traffic accident causalities due to the unsafe condition of vehicles used by smugglers. (Often smugglers rig the vehicles to hide as many aliens as possible, making the vehicle unsafe to operate.)[102] Some border deaths are tied to smuggling, as some smugglers mislead their charges about how far it is to the United States and how much water is needed to make the journey.[103]

Alien smuggling-related activities may be prosecuted under a variety of criminal statutes including immigration document fraud and bribery.[104] In addition, other federal crimes may be applicable as alien smuggling is listed among the Racketeer Influence and Corrupt Organization (RICO)[105] predicate offenses and is included in the definition of specified unlawful activities for money laundering statutes.[106] Furthermore, criminal and civil forfeiture statues[107] may apply to alien smuggling cases. From October to March FY2005, ICE reported the seizure of $7.8 million from alien smuggling investigations.

DHS' Role in the Anti-Smuggling Effort

Under the INS, two separate entities in the organization, the border patrol (USBP) and the INS investigations program, conducted alien smuggling investigations. The Government Accountability Office (GAO) found that due to a lack of program coordination between the two INS entities, there were several anti-smuggling units that overlapped in their jurisdictions, operated autonomously, and reported to different officials.[108] The abolishment of the INS and the transfer of its functions to DHS may have resolved some of these issues. According to an ICE Office of Investigations (OI) official, the border patrol has a minor role in alien smuggling and trafficking and is required to coordinate with OI before initiating anti-smuggling investigations.[109] Nonetheless, it is unclear that this coordination is functioning smoothly. (Recently a sting was compromised because of lack of coordination between ICE and CBP when ICE agents were trying to cross the border with money and drugs to uncover the entire smuggling operation.)[110]

ICE's Anti-Smuggling Role

ICE works to identify and dismantle large-scale transnational smuggling organizations in collaboration with other law enforcement agencies, both foreign and domestic. Major investigations are conducted with the cooperation and assistance of other federal, state, and local law enforcement agencies, as well as the appropriate bureaus of foreign governments.[111] ICE reports that it coordinates the anti-smuggling efforts of all divisions in DHS, including investigations offices, overseas offices, inspections at ports-of-entry (POEs), and Border Patrol units between POEs.[112] It is also the primary DHS component for investigating alien smuggling, but Customs and Border Protection (CBP) and the U.S Coast Guard are also involved.

ICE is developing a foreign and domestic strategy to combat alien smuggling which includes implementing critical incident response teams, and using the money laundering statutes and the identification and seizure of assets and criminal proceeds to strip away the assets and profit incentive of smuggling organizations.[113] Nonetheless, reportedly ICE has not finalized its strategy for combating alien smuggling. Begun in summer 2003 — soon after the formation of DHS — the strategy is being adjusted to focus on the southwest border and to encompass the smuggling of aliens, drugs, and other contraband.[114]

ICE places a significant emphasis on targeting alien smuggling organizations that present threats to national security, recognizing that terrorists are likely to align themselves with alien smuggling networks to obtain undetected entry into the United States.[115] It is widely believed that there are factors which have created an environment in which terrorist and smuggling enterprises may combine their criminal efforts to pose a significant threat to national security. These factors include the increase in sophistication of criminal organizations, the ability of these organizations to exploit public corruption, and the lax immigration controls in transit countries. In addition, smuggling pipelines that are used by unauthorized aliens and criminals seeking to enter the United States could also be used by terrorists to gain entrance into the United States.[116] DHS' global Anti-Smuggling/Human Trafficking Strategy concentrates efforts on intelligence-driven investigations against major violators, specifically targeting organizations with ties to countries that support terrorist organizations such as al Qaeda.[117]

CBP's Anti-Smuggling Role

The U.S. Border Patrol (USBP) in CBP is responsible for interdicting aliens smuggled between ports of entry. Generally, after the USBP makes an interdiction, the smuggled aliens are separated from members of the smuggling organization; interviews are conducted of both groups; sworn statements are solicited from material witnesses; fingerprints are taken; and other relevant information is accumulated. CBP refers to ICE's Office of Investigations only those cases that involve a significant scope, violence, or other egregious circumstances. The USBP also makes referrals to ICE based on more in-depth or strategic analyses conducted by USBP's intelligence units which routinely analyze alien-smuggling interdictions to develop information on smuggling patterns and identify leads warranting further investigation.[118]

ICE and CBP Smuggling Memorandum of Understanding

A recent GAO report noted that the effectiveness of ICE's anti-smuggling strategy would depend partly on the clarification of the ICE and CBP's roles in anti-smuggling activities. In April 2004, ICE and CBP signed a Memorandum of Understanding (MOU) which stated that,

- ICE would assume the full burden of administratively supporting, equipping, and funding the anti-smuggling units.
- ICE would have lead responsibility for certain nationally designated cases as well as Joint Terrorism Task Force cases.
- USBP would have responsibility for border-related interdiction activities, including checkpoint operations.
- USBP and ICE would be jointly responsible for ensuring the proper and timely sharing of information and intelligence.
- There is a need to develop a more comprehensive agreement regarding the working relationship between ICE investigations and CBP.

In November 2004, ICE and CBP signed a second MOU addressing the bureaus' roles and responsibilities, including provisions for sharing information and intelligence. The MOU reiterated that ICE's Office of Investigations has primary responsibility for all investigations, while the USBP has primary responsibility for interdictions between ports of entry. Nonetheless, the MOU stated that the missions of the two bureaus "are intricately connected and complementary."[119] However, at this time, there is no mechanism for tracking the status of cases referred to ICE by CBP, which may cause the agency to miss opportunities to identify and investigate large smuggling operations.[120] In addition, there have reportedly been communications issues between ICE and CBP during some smuggling investigations.[121]

The Role of Other Federal Agencies

Other federal agencies, including the Department of Justice's Criminal Division, Federal Bureau of Investigation, U.S. Attorney's Office, Department of Treasury's Internal Revenue Service's Criminal Division, and the Financial Crimes Enforcement Network (FinCEN), play a role in combating alien smuggling. Likewise, since alien smuggling and document fraud are often linked, the Department of State's Bureau of Diplomatic Security also is involved in the anti-smuggling effort due to its mission to protect travel documents. Additionally, the Department of State's Bureau of International Narcotics and Law Enforcement Affairs coordinates international anti-smuggling efforts (e.g., helping countries draft alien smuggling legislation, providing funds to foreign countries that have intercepted smuggled aliens to assist in returning these aliens to their home countries). The Central Intelligence Agency's (CIA) Office of Transnational Issues provides analytical assessments related to alien smuggling, and the Department of Defense's National Security Agency (NSA) assists in the interdiction of smuggled aliens overseas.[122]

Human Smuggling and Trafficking Center

The Human Smuggling and Trafficking Center (HSTC) is an interagency group — including the Departments of Justice, State, and Homeland Security — which provides information to counter migrant smuggling, trafficking of persons, and clandestine terrorist travel. The center's three primary objectives are (1) prevention and deterrence of smuggling and related trafficking activities, (2) investigation and prosecution of the criminals involved in such activity, and (3) protection of and assistance for victims as provided in applicable law and policy.[123]

Selected Alien Smuggling Issues

The number of individuals smuggled into the United States has increased dramatically, and smuggling organizations have become more sophisticated. Furthermore, there were concerns about the former INS' ability to combat alien smuggling, and it is unknown how many of these problems carried over into ICE. For example, the INS lacked the field intelligence staff to collect and analyze information on alien smuggling.[124] In addition, a 2000 GAO report noted the lack of program coordination and the absence of an automated case management system as impeding anti-smuggling efforts.[125]

Nonetheless, the ability of DHS to combine alien smuggling and money laundering investigations reportedly has aided in alien smuggling investigations. ICE has the ability to pursue money laundering charges related to smuggling since DHS has the authorities of the former U.S. Customs Service. This capacity did not exist in INS, and INS would have had to seek outside assistance to pursue additional charges.[126] On the other hand, there have been reports of a lack of coordination on alien smuggling between ICE and CBP which has lead to inefficiencies in alien smuggling investigations.

Smuggling or Humanitarian Assistance

The line between humanitarian assistance and alien smuggling is not always clearly defined. In 1986, the Reverend John Fife was convicted of alien smuggling for his work in the "sanctuary movement," providing shelter to illegal aliens from

Central American, most of whom were fleeing civil wars.[127] In July 2005, two volunteers from the group No More Deaths, which provides water and medical care to unauthorized aliens crossing the Arizona desert, were arrested and charged with alien smuggling. According to the volunteers, they were transporting three unauthorized aliens to a church in Tucson, Arizona to provide medical care. Nonetheless, the aliens were being transported in furtherance of their unlawful presence, and the group did not intend to notify USBP.[128]

In addition, the group Humane Borders sets up water stations in the desert for aliens trying to cross illegally into the United States and recently printed a map of the routes through the Arizona desert into the United States, illustrating USBP beacons, Humane Borders water stations, and migrant places of death. According to the group, the objective of the maps is to try to dissuade migrants from undertaking an illegal border crossing by warning them of the risks. However, others argue that Humane Borders is aiding and abetting illegal entry, and is engaging in alien smuggling.[129]

Immigration Fraud

Defining Immigration Fraud[130]

Immigration fraud is generally grouped into two types — immigration-related document fraud and immigration benefit fraud.

- Immigration-related document fraud includes the counterfeiting, sale and/or use of identity documents or "breeder documents" (i.e., documents used to confirm identity, such as birth certificates or Social Security cards),[131] as well as alien registration documents and stamps, employment authorizations, passports, visas, or any documents used to circumvent immigration laws.
- Benefit fraud encompasses the willful misrepresentation of a material fact to obtain an immigration benefit in the absence of lawful eligibility for that benefit.[132]

Some view immigration fraud as a continuum of events because people may commit document fraud en route to benefit fraud.

The INA addresses immigration fraud in several ways. First, the law makes "misrepresentation" (e.g., obtaining a visa by falsely representing a material fact or entering the United States by falsely claiming U.S. citizenship) a ground for inadmissibility.[133] Second, the INA has civil enforcement provisions, distinct from removal or inadmissibility proceedings, to prosecute individuals and entities that engage in immigration document fraud.[134]

In addition to the INA, §1546 of the U.S. Criminal Code makes it a criminal offense for a person to knowingly produce, use, or facilitate the production or use of fraudulent immigration documents such as visas, border crossing cards, and other documents covered by immigration-related statute or regulation. The U.S. Criminal Code furthermore criminalizes immigration fraud pertaining to the knowing falsification of naturalization, citizenship, or alien registry. More generally, the U.S. Criminal Code criminalizes the knowing commission of fraud in connection with a wide range of identification documents.[135]

Measuring Fraud

Immigration fraud is reportedly widespread, though estimates of its pervasiveness are not available.[136] The conventional wisdom is that document fraud increased following the enactment of the Immigration Reform and Control Act of 1986, which first required employers to inspect the documents of prospective employees.[137] Large-scale black market enterprises providing counterfeit immigration documents and "breeder" documents developed to supply unauthorized alien workers with necessary papers. Given that calculations based upon the 2005 Current Population Survey estimated that 11.1 million aliens were residing in the United States without legal authorization, it is reasonable to presume that many of these unauthorized aliens are committing document fraud. Nonimmigrant visa fraud among aliens temporarily in the United States has also been an ongoing problem.[138] It is possible that many of those people who broker in immigration fraud are legal residents or citizens of the United States.

Many policy analysts maintain that the pervasiveness of immigration fraud facilitates the entry and assimilation of those aliens who pose threats to the United States. The National Commission on Terrorist Attacks Upon the United States (commonly known as the 9/11 Commission) showed that several of 19 hijackers responsible for the 9/11 attacks were able to obtain visas to enter the United States through the use of forged documents. Incomplete intelligence and screening enabled many of the hijackers to enter the United States despite flaws in their entry documents or suspicions regarding their past associations. According to the 9/11 Commission, up to 15 of the hijackers could have been intercepted or deported through more diligent enforcement of immigration laws.[139]

Investigating Fraud

The types of fraud investigations range in circumstances and scope. Many investigations focus on facilitators, i.e., those who sell, distribute or manufacture counterfeit or altered documents and on criminal organizations that broker large-scale illegal schemes such as sham marriage rings or bogus job offers. Investigations of immigration benefit applications are another major activity.

As immigration enforcement strategies have changed and resources have shifted over time, it has long been evident that investigations of immigration fraud has declined as a priority. In FY1986, for example, the productive workyears devoted to fraud investigation reportedly equaled 256 special agents, and they completed 11,316 fraud cases. Ten years later (FY1995), there were 181 special agent workyears, and they completed only 6,455 cases.[140] When the INS issued its "Interior Enforcement Strategy" in 1999, however, minimizing immigration benefit fraud and other document abuse was listed as the fourth among five top priorities.[141]

Evaluations of the government's efforts to combat immigration benefit fraud and document abuse have generally been critical.[142] GAO noted that "INS did not believe it had sufficient staff to reach its program goals." GAO also reported that benefit fraud investigations were hampered by a lack of integrated information systems. "The operations units at the four INS service centers that investigate benefit fraud operate different information systems that did not interface with each other or with the units that investigate benefit fraud at INS district offices. ... Thus, INS was not in the best position to review numerous applications and detect patterns, trends, and potential schemes for benefit fraud."[143]

Staffing of Fraud Investigations

The cuts in fraud investigations between FY1992 and FY2003 appear to have been generally across the board in terms of types of investigations pursued. As Figure 8 depicts, workyears spent investigating facilitators of counterfeit or altered documents, organizations that broker large-scale illegal schemes and persons suspected of immigration benefit fraud have all decreased. Note that the "all other" category in FY2003 includes the investigations of civil violations of document fraud (INA §274C) that were enacted in1996, and likely account for its relative increase.

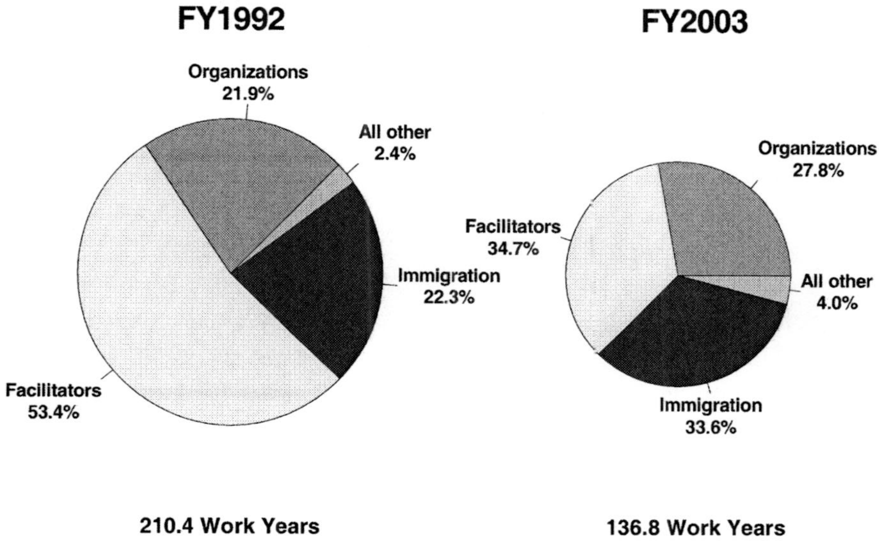

Source: CRS analysis of DHS Office of Immigration Statistics PAS data.

Figure 8. Fraud Investigations by Type or Target, FY1992 and FY2003.

Selected Fraud Issues

There appears to be a continued lack of coordination between U.S. Citizenship and Immigration Services (USCIS) and ICE in the area of fraud and national security investigations.[144] USCIS established the Office of Fraud Detection and National Security to work with the appropriate law enforcement entities to handle national security and criminal "hits" on aliens and to identify systemic fraud in the application process. Many of these duties were formerly performed by the INS enforcement arm that is now part of ICE. The GAO has reported, "The difficulty between USCIS and ICE investigations regarding benefit fraud is not new.... As a result, some USCIS field officials told us that ICE would not pursue single cases of benefit fraud. ICE field officials who spoke on this issue cited a lack of investigative resources as to why they could not respond in the manner USCIS wanted."[145]

The inter-agency coordination problems, coupled with the observable decline in investigator work years allocated to document and benefit fraud, are more relevant when considering the role bogus documents and benefit fraud play in facilitating other violations of law. Some maintain that limited enforcement resources should not be spent going after purveyors who primarily are providing false identification so that unauthorized aliens can work. Others argue that it is critical to investigate the black market in counterfeit documents and benefit fraud because it is especially important to international terrorists, organized crime syndicates, and alien smuggling rings — all of whom rely on fraudulent documents to minimize detection.

Worksite Enforcement

The INA prohibits the unlawful employment of aliens and related discrimination.[146] These prohibitions were added to the INA by the Immigration Reform and Control Act of 1986 (IRCA). The provisions on unlawful employment sought to deter unauthorized immigration by reducing the magnet of employment. These provisions, as amended, make it unlawful for an employer to knowingly hire, or recruit or refer for a fee, or continue to employ an alien who is not authorized to be so employed. They require employers to verify the employment eligibility of new hires by examining documents that establish identity and work eligibility, and to complete and retain verification forms. Employers violating these requirements may be subject to civil and/or criminal penalties, known as employer sanctions.[147] The term employer sanctions is also used generally to refer to the provisions on unlawful employment. The ICE Office of Investigations has primary responsibility for enforcing these provisions. The related anti-discrimination provisions, as amended, prohibit employment discrimination against U.S. citizens or work-authorized aliens based on national origin or on citizenship or immigration status. These provisions are enforced by the Office of Special Counsel for Immigration-Related Unfair Employment Practices (OSC) in the Civil Rights Division of the U.S. Department of Justice.[148]

Full enforcement of the employer sanctions provisions began in June 1988 in the nonagricultural sector and in December 1988 in agriculture. Primary enforcement responsibility at the time rested with the former INS as part of its investigations program[149] In the early years, educating employers about their responsibilities in order to promote voluntary compliance continued to be a key focus of the program. At the same time, an increasing emphasis was placed on enforcing penalties against violators. At that time, enforcement of employer sanctions combined "traditional investigations — based on leads about suspected violations — with compliance investigations based on neutral, or random, selection of employers."[150]

Policy Changes

Policies governing the enforcement of employer sanctions have changed over the years. On April 5, 1991, then-INS Commissioner Gene McNary issued a memorandum ordering the Office of Enforcement and the Office of the General Counsel to launch a six-month initiative to strengthen enforcement of employer sanctions.[151] An implementation plan accompanying the memorandum stated: "The message to employers must be unequivocal — INS is prepared to vigorously enforce administrative and criminal sanctions against those who violate the law." According to the implementation plan, INS investigators were to spend at least 30 percent of their time for the remainder of FY1991 on each of three investigations program priorities — employer sanctions, criminal aliens, and fraud. New fraud cases were to focus predominantly on employer sanctions-related fraud. In addition, INS worksite enforcement resources were to be directed toward enforcement activities and not used for employer education.[152] In January 1992, the enhanced worksite enforcement initiative was extended indefinitely.

In February 1995, President Clinton issued a memorandum which identified worksite enforcement and employer sanctions as a major component of the Administration's overall strategy to deter illegal immigration. The Administration's approach was to "target enforcement efforts at employers and industries that historically have relied upon employment of illegal immigrants." [153]

For FY1996, the Clinton Administration requested, and Congress appropriated, significant funding increases for interior enforcement, including worksite enforcement and employment eligibility verification. At that time, Congress also enacted the Illegal Immigration Reform and Immigrant Responsibility Act of 1996 (IIRIRA), which established three pilot programs for employment eligibility confirmation; reduced the number of acceptable documents for purposes of completing employment eligibility verification forms, known as I-9 forms; and provided employers with the possibility of a "good faith" defense against technical violations of I-9 requirements.[154] During the 1995-1998 period, INS conducted numerous onsite workplace raids and arrested thousands of unauthorized aliens.

In 1998, INS changed its approach to worksite enforcement.[155] Apparently, the change was prompted largely by complaints about INS tactics during worksite raids. The new procedures responded to complaints by Congress and others, and incorporated the "best practices" of various offices.[156] An INS memorandum at that time noted that "worksite enforcement operations [actions by INS to arrest unauthorized aliens at a worksite] are sometimes misunderstood by the general public" leading to a lack of public support.[157] Given that the "purpose of worksite enforcement is to deter the unlawful employment of aliens... worksite enforcement investigations that involve alien smuggling, human rights abuses, and other criminal violations must take precedence."[158]

As discussed above, in 1999, INS unveiled a new interior enforcement strategy, which included five priorities, two of which related to worksite enforcement. In a prepared statement for a July 1999 hearing by the House Judiciary Committee's Subcommittee on Immigration and Claims, INS Executive Associate Commissioner for Policy and Planning Robert Bach explained the relationship between these two worksite enforcement priorities as follows:

> INS believes there is a clear nexus between defeating smuggling organizations — which is Priority 2 — and blocking access to and removing undocumented workers — Priority 5. Disrupting and dismantling a smuggling organization that transports undocumented workers across the U.S. border will have a direct impact on limiting employers' access to this exploitable source of labor. Additionally, anti-smuggling efforts generate leads on employers and industries employing undocumented workers.[159]

According to Bach, the new interior enforcement strategy emphasized both working cooperatively with employers to improve their compliance with employment eligibility verification requirements and reduce unauthorized employment, as well as prosecuting employers who violate the law. He indicated that INS would focus on criminal employer cases, cases in which there was a pattern or practice of knowingly employing unauthorized workers, and would target, in particular, employers who abused their workers and who violated multiple laws.[160]

Under the 1999 interior enforcement strategy, INS pursued the general tactical approach of auditing I-9 forms to identify suspected unauthorized aliens. It did so on a large-scale basis in an operation targeting the meatpacking industry, called "Operation Vanguard." Launched in the fall of 1998, Operation Vanguard involved subpoenaing the I-9 forms and other employment records of workers in all the meatpacking plants in Nebraska and in some plants in Iowa and South Dakota. By checking these records against INS, Social Security Administration, and other databases, INS developed lists of employees whose work authorization it could not verify. These lists were then distributed to employers, who arranged interviews for the workers with INS.

At the July 1999 House Immigration and Claims Subcommittee hearing, Mark Reed, then director of the INS Central Region office, maintained that the Operation Vanguard approach was more effective than the workplace raids and arrests of past years:

> If the numbers were smaller, if we had less people in the United States unlawfully, if we had less employers engaging in this, doing raids and removing people would be a much more effective strategy, but we simply can't do that.[161]

Operation Vanguard prompted a strong political backlash, however, and was ended. Testifying at a May 2005 joint hearing by the Senate Judiciary Committee's Subcommittees on Immigration, Border Security, and Citizenship and Terrorism, Technology, and Homeland Security, Reed, now with a consulting firm, offered his retrospective views on Operation Vanguard:

> Vanguard demonstrated an efficient and effective capability to bar unauthorized workers from employment in any given sector. When the capability was realized, it was stopped as well. In reality, the implementation of Vanguard was not good government.... Depriving these [meatpacking] plants the ability to remain competitive was a major threat to the livelihood of everyone in the community.

In the aftermath of the September 11, 2001 attacks, interior enforcement resources were redirected from traditional program areas, including worksite enforcement, to national security-related investigations. While criminal employer cases remained a stated priority of the worksite enforcement program, they became subordinate to "removing unauthorized workers from critical infrastructure facilities such as airports, military bases, research facilities, nuclear plants, etc."[162] A 2003 memorandum issued by ICE headquarters suggests the extent of the post-9/11 emphasis on critical infrastructure investigations. The memorandum requires field offices to request headquarters approval before opening a worksite enforcement investigation not related to critical infrastructure protection.[163]

Coordination with Department of Labor

While ICE has primary responsibility for enforcing INA provisions on the unlawful employment of aliens, the Department of Labor (DOL) also has a role. The INA requires that employers retain completed I-9 employment eligibility verification forms and make them available for inspection by DOL. In addition to this statutory role, it is widely believed that DOL, specifically the Employment Standards Administration (ESA), can help reduce unauthorized employment by carrying out its core responsibilities to enforce labor standards. Enforcing labor standards can help deter unauthorized employment, it is argued, by depriving employers of some of the potential financial advantages of employing unauthorized workers at substandard wages and working conditions.

In 1992, INS and DOL's ESA entered into a memorandum of understanding (MOU) to improve cooperation and coordination between the agencies.[164] Under the terms of the 1992 MOU, ESA was given authority to issue warning notices to employers for violations of the employment eligibility verification requirements. ESA also was to promptly refer suspected substantive violations to INS. At the same time, the MOU stated that ESA, would not take any action which would compromise its ability to carry out its fundamental mission [of enforcing labor standards statutes], regardless of the workers' immigration status. DOL officials took the position that investigating worksite immigration matters, beyond reviewing I-9 forms, could impede their efforts to enforce worker protection laws.[165] Thus, ESA's role was limited mainly to reviewing employers' I-9 forms and reporting results to INS.

ESA and INS signed a new MOU in 1998 that sought to address DOL's concerns about conducting worksite immigration enforcement and to clarify the enforcement roles and responsibilities of each agency.[166] Under the 1998 MOU, ESA investigators are to inspect employer compliance with I-9 requirements in conjunction with labor standards enforcement only in directed investigations, that is, investigations not based on complaints. According to the MOU, this limitation "is intended and will be implemented so as to avoid discouraging complaints from unauthorized workers who may be victims of labor standards violations by their employer." During these compliance inspections, ESA investigators are not to make inquiries about workers' immigration status and are not to issue warning notices or Notices of Intent to Fine. ESA is to promptly refer to INS all suspected serious violations uncovered during directed investigations. While this MOU remains in effect, it is of less relevance at the present time in light of ICE's current worksite enforcement focus on critical infrastructure facilities.

Program Performance

As discussed above, employers who violate INA provisions on the unlawful employment of aliens may be subject to civil and/or criminal penalties. For violations of I-9 paperwork requirements or of the prohibition against knowingly hiring or continuing to employ aliens who lack employment authorization, employers may be subject to fines. If ICE believes that an employer has committed a violation of these provisions, the agency may issue the employer a Notice of Intent to Fine (NIF). A NIF may result in a Final Order for civil money penalties, a settlement, or a dismissal.[167] Employers convicted of having engaged in a pattern or practice of knowingly hiring or continuing to employ unauthorized aliens may face fines and/or imprisonment.[168]

Table 1. Worksite Enforcement Program Performance: FY1999-FY2003

Fiscal Year	FY1999	FY2000	FY2001	FY2002	FY2003
Criminal Employer Cases Presented for Prosecution	182	109	239	21	4
Notices of Intent to Fine (NIFs) Issued	443	213	141	73	16
Fine Amounts Collected	$3,690,575	$2,234,181	$1,599,323	$509,835	$212,322

Source: CRS Presentation of DHS data. The data on fine collections are from the DHS Debt Management Center; the other data are from the LYNX database.

Table 1 provides data on worksite enforcement program performance for FY1999 through FY2003.[169] As shown, the number of NIFs issued and the amount of fine collections decreased steadily during this period. Policy changes and reallocations of resources can help explain these trends. As discussed above, INS's 1999 interior enforcement strategy de-emphasized non-criminal employer cases, which can generate administrative fines, in favor of criminal cases. In accordance with this strategy, "criminal employer cases presented for prosecution" became the only worksite enforcement program production quota assigned to INS field offices in FY1999.[170]

In light of the priority given to criminal prosecutions, however, the significant decrease from FY1999 to FY2000 in this measure is puzzling. The decreases in the three measures between FY2001 and FY2002 presumably reflect, at least in part, the post-September 11, 2001 redirection of enforcement resources toward national security-related investigations. Underreporting may also have contributed to these decreases, especially the sharp drops in "criminal cases presented for prosecution." According to ICE, data for FY2002 and FY2003 may understate actual activity.

While the availability of resources and policy shifts help explain changes in worksite enforcement program performance over time, the program also faces more perennial challenges that impact performance. Among these challenges are the applicable legal standards for sanctioning employers and the prevalence of fraudulent documents. INA §274A makes it unlawful for employers to knowingly hire or continue to employ unauthorized aliens. Under the law, an employer is required to attest that he or she has verified that an employee is not unauthorized to work by examining documentation provided by the employee. An employer is considered to be in compliance with this examination requirement "if the document reasonably appears on its face to be genuine." INA §274A also provides that an employer who establishes that he or she has complied in good faith with the I-9 requirements has an affirmative defense against the charge of knowingly hiring an unauthorized alien. The widespread availability and use of fraudulent documents[171] makes it difficult to prove that an employer knowingly hired an unauthorized alien and, thus, should be subject to penalties. With respect to sanctions for violations of the I-9 requirements, a 1996 amendment to INA §274A provides employers with the possibility of a good faith defense against technical or procedural violations.

Current Policy Issues and Options

Worksite enforcement is a current focus of congressional interest. Among the reasons for this is the large and growing unauthorized alien population, the majority of whom are in the labor force. According to estimates by the Pew Hispanic Center, in 2004 the unauthorized alien population totaled about 10.3 million and the unauthorized alien working population totaled about 6.3 million.[172] Particularly since the 2001 terrorist attacks, security concerns have been raised about having such a large unauthorized population.

In addition, the issue of worksite enforcement has gained attention recently in connection with guest worker proposals. In January 2004, President Bush outlined a proposal for a new temporary worker program, and called for increased workplace enforcement as part of the program.[173] As Congress turns its attention to worksite enforcement, there are several key policy issues it may opt to consider:

Resources

Historically, as discussed above, investigative time devoted to employer cases has been limited. In the aftermath of the 2001 terrorist attacks, resources available for worksite enforcement further dwindled, as interior enforcement increasingly focused on national security investigations. Policy questions include whether additional personnel or other resources would improve the performance of the worksite enforcement program and whether such resources should be provided.

Employment Eligibility Verification

Related to worksite enforcement and its goal of reducing unauthorized employment is the process of employment eligibility verification. Under the mandatory I-9 system, employers examine documents to verify a new hire's identity and work authorization, and employers and employees complete I-9 forms. There is broad agreement that the widespread availability and use of fraudulent documents has largely undermined the I-9 system. Another available mechanism for employment eligibility verification is the Basic Pilot program, in which participating employers electronically verify new hires' I-9 information through Social Security Administration and CIS databases to determine whether individuals are authorized to work. The Basic Pilot program is now available nationwide and participation is, for the most part, voluntary.[174] Policy questions include whether to revise or replace the current verification systems. Options under discussion include making the Basic Pilot program mandatory for some subset of, or all, employers, and requiring job seekers to have some type of tamper-proof work authorization document. These and other options may, in turn, raise concerns about privacy and discrimination.

Employer Sanctions

Another policy question concerns whether the current penalties for employers who violate the law on the unlawful employment of aliens should be changed. Some have argued that employer sanctions and the prohibition against hiring unauthorized aliens should be repealed entirely, on the grounds that they have not succeeded in curbing unauthorized employment and have had other negative effects, such as lowering wages and undercutting efforts to improve working conditions. Others have argued, alternatively, that existing penalties should be raised and vigorously enforced to increase their deterrent effect.

Some have argued that worksite enforcement has never been truly implemented as employer sanctions were never systematically enforced. The former INS conducted few inspections and they were generally performed randomly instead of targeting industries that were most likely to hire unauthorized aliens.[175]

Role of Other Federal Agencies in Worksite Enforcement

There are other federal agencies which could play a larger role in aiding DHS's worksite enforcement efforts. The most obvious agencies who could aid in worksite enforcement are the Department of Labor (DOL), since many argue that those who commit wage and hour violations are also likely to use unauthorized alien labor, and Social Security Administration (SSA), since the agency can detect possible fraudulent uses of social security numbers (SSN's). However, increasing the immigration enforcement role of other federal agencies is controversial and could distract the agencies from their primary missions. GAO has testified that coordination between the INS and with other federal agencies was sometimes problematic, noting that the Department of Labor (DOL) was hesitant to delve into work authorization issues as it might cause workers to fail to report potential wage and safety violations.[176]

In addition, recently ICE has been criticized for impersonating other federal agencies to locate unauthorized aliens. For example, in 2005, ICE agents conducted an operation by pretending to be from the Occupational Safety and Health Administration (OSHA), and tricking workers into attending a "mandatory training session." The operation was successful, leading to the arrest of 48 unauthorized workers, but was also criticized by the DOL, local officials, and immigration and job safety advocates, who argued that the operation could cause immigrant workers to distrust safety officials responsible for protecting the workers by reducing injury rates.[177]

Department of Labor

Discussing the MOU at the July 1999 House hearing, John Fraser, then Deputy Administrator of ESA's Wage and Hour Division, described "the fundamental dilemma of worksite enforcement" for DOL:

> DOL needs the cooperation of workers, including undocumented workers, to report on labor standards violations or provide information needed to develop enforcement cases. Unfortunately, many vulnerable low-wage workers — the primary focus of DOL labor standards enforcement — are often much less willing to report workplace exploitation or cooperate in DOL investigations when they perceive that doing so threatens their continued employment either because of retaliation by their employer or because contact with DOL could trigger an INS action to deport them, their family or their friends.[178]

As discussed above, in 1998 and 1999, the INS experimented with alternative raids called Operation Vanguard, using SSA's work records to identify unauthorized aliens rather than conducting worksite raids. Operation Vangaurd did not result in many deportations, but may have worked as a deterrent, reducing the desirability of the meat packing industry to unauthorized aliens. Nonetheless, Operation Vangaurd was criticized by workers, farmers, and industry leaders for violating workers' privacy rights and targeting Hispanics. In 1999, SSA stopped allowing INS to check employee records against their database, citing privacy concerns, unless INS has "reasonable cause to believe that a worker is unauthorized.[179]

Mark Krikorian, Executive Director of the Center of Immigration Studies, testified that in the late 1990's the INS received criticism for worksite enforcement in Nebraska's meat packing plants and Georgia's onion fields. As a result, it developed a new interior enforcement strategy which focused entirely on criminal aliens and smugglers.[180]

Social Security Administration (SSA)

SSA has data which could be used to aid DHS in the identification of unauthorized alien workers. For example, SSA maintains a Nonwork Alien File which contains social security numbers (SSNs) issued to aliens without work authorization. Earnings posted to numbers in the Nonwork Alien File might indicate that an alien is working without authorization. However, the alien may have received work authorization after the nonwork SSN was issued. DHS has said that the agency would have to invest significant resources to determine whether the alien is working without authorization, and that this use of resources may not be cost effective and would pull resources from other national security-related initiatives. In addition, neither SSA nor DHS can easily update work status, since their records lack a common identifier.[181]

In addition to data issues, there may be public resistance to SSA increasing their role in the enforcement of immigration laws. For example, in 2002, a policy change at SSA that substantially increased the number of "no-match" letters sent to employers received much attention due to its impact on unauthorized aliens. No-match letters are sent to employers to inform them of a discrepancy between a W-2 form and SSA's records, so that workers can be properly credited with their earnings, and to combat identity fraud. Importantly, receipt of a no-match letter does not imply that the employee is using a fraudulent SSN; the discrepancy could be the result of a clerical error. For tax years 1993 through 2000, an employer only received no-match letters if 10 or more employees had discrepancies and the number of employees with mismatches equaled at least 10% of the employer's workforce.[182]

For the 2001 tax year, SSA implemented a new policy of sending no-match letters to every employer with at least one employee with discrepancies on his or her W-2. For tax year 2000, SSA sent out approximately 110,000 no-match letters[183] compared to approximately 950,000 for tax year 2001. However, the result was an increase in complaints from employers who did not understand the purpose of the no-match letter. In addition, immigration advocates contend that tens of thousands of aliens left their jobs or were fired as a result of the letters.[184] Due to the controversy, SSA again changed their policy, sending out approximately 110,000 no-match letters for tax year 2002.[185]

Immigration Enforcement at Ports of Entry: Immigration Inspections [186]

The Immigration and Nationality Act (INA) requires the inspection of all aliens who seek entry into the United States[187] and in some cases at a preinspection site in a foreign country.[188] The purpose of the inspection is to determine the admissibility of a traveler to the United States. Section 287 of the INA enumerates the following authorities for immigration officers, including immigration inspectors:

- to question under oath any person seeking to enter the United States in order to determine admissibility, and
- to search, without warrant, the person and belongings of any applicant seeking admission.[189]

The majority of immigration inspections take place during the *primary* inspections process. Primary inspections is the first level of inspection, which consists of a brief interview with an inspector, a cursory check of the traveler's documents, and a query of the Interagency Border Inspection System (IBIS). Primary inspections are quick (usually lasting no longer than a minute), however, if the inspector is suspicious that the traveler may be in violation of the INA or other U.S. laws, the traveler is referred to a secondary inspection.

During *secondary* inspections, aliens are questioned extensively and travel documents are further examined. Several immigration databases are queried as well, including lookout databases.[190] The majority of travelers, however, are not subject to a secondary inspection.

In addition to conducting inspections, immigration inspectors enforce various criminal and immigration statutes. For example, immigration inspectors are on the front line with respect to intercepting fraudulent documents used by aliens as well as intercepting aliens, drugs, weapons and explosives that are smuggled into the United States. Immigration inspectors also encounter criminal aliens who attempt to gain entry into the United States. While immigration inspectors may encounter enforcement-related issues during primary inspections, it is during secondary inspections that immigration inspectors conduct enforcement-related activities. In FY2003, immigration inspectors spent 13% of their time on enforcement-related activities.[191] Over the most recent four years for which data are available, the time spent by immigration inspectors on enforcement activities has steadily risen, with the exception of FY2001 when it dropped 3% from FY2000 (see Figure 9 and Table 2).

Table 2. Percentage of Inspector Hours Spent on Primary and Secondary Inspections and Enforcement Activities: FY1992-FY2003

	Primary	Secondary	Enforce		Primary	Secondary	Enforce
1992	69.20%	28.6%	2.1%	1998	62.2%	30.9%	6.8%
1993	69%	28.9%	2.1%	1999	63.4%	29.5%	7.1%
1994	68.4%	29.5%	2.1%	2000	63.4%	27.4%	9.2%
1995	65.3%	29.2%	5.5%	2001	69.8%	24.1%	6.1%
1996	65.4%	30.4%	4.2%	2002	68.2%	20.8%	11%
1997	63.2%	31.5%	5.3%	2003	65.3%	21.8%	12.9%

Source: CRS Analysis of data from DHS's Performance Analysis System (PAS).

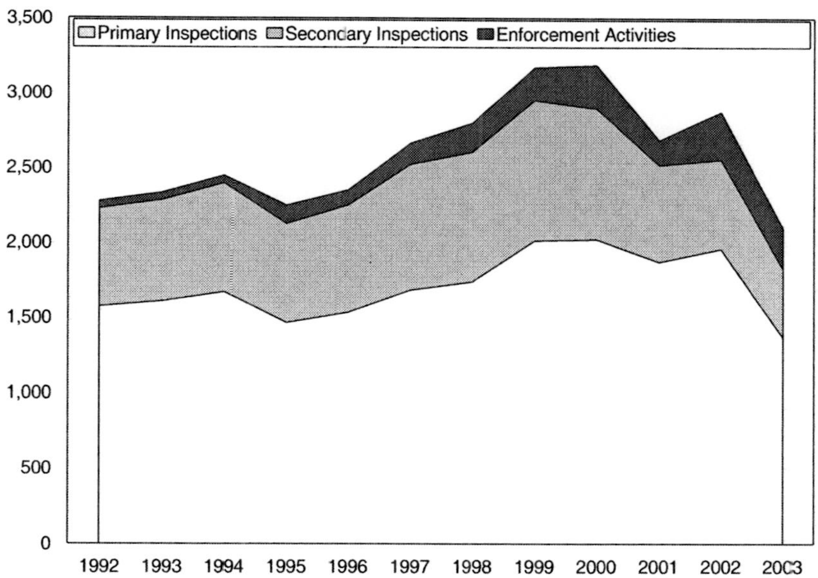

	1992	1993	1994	1995	1996	1997	1998	1999	2000	2001	2002	2003
Enforcement Activities	48.5	49.3	51	123.3	98.9	140.9	190.9	224.6	294.3	164.5	315.8	270.7
Secondary Inspections	650.4	673.7	722.6	656.6	713.8	839.2	865	936.1	872.5	645.7	596	456.8
Primary Inspections	1,574	1,608.4	1,672.5	1,465	1,536.2	1,684.8	1,740	2,013	2,021.8	1,873.3	1,959.8	1,370.5
Total Workyears	**2,272.9**	**2,331.3**	**2,446.1**	**2,244.9**	**2,348.9**	**2,664.9**	**2,795.9**	**3,173.7**	**3,188.6**	**2,683.5**	**2,871.6**	**2,098**

Source: CRS Analysis of data from DHS's Performance Analysis System (PAS).

Figure 9. Inspector Workyears by Type: FY1992-FY2003.

Immigration inspectors generate cases that are referred to ICE's investigative unit for investigation and prosecution.[192] An analysis of the data shows that the number of cases that were referred to investigations during the period that was analyzed peaked in 2002, at 1,782 cases (see Table 3). In FY2003, the number of cases referred to investigations dropped 42% from FY2002, to 1,028 cases.

Table 3. Immigration Inspections: Cases Referred to Investigations for Prosecution and Interception of Smuggled Aliens, Narcotics, and Contraband: FY2000-FY2003

Year	Cases referred	Intercepted Aliens	Intercepted narcotics	Intercepted contraband
2000	636	19,857	3,764	N.A.
2001	1,676	31,261	4,892	320
2002	1,782	32,173	3,913	945
2003	1,028	34,473	1,988	1,359

Source: CRS analysis of PAS data.

Note: Contraband includes weapons and explosives. Data on contraband not available for FY2002.

Interception of Smuggled Goods

Immigration inspectors play a key role in intercepting the smuggling of humans, narcotics and contraband. The interception of aliens that are smuggled into the United States led all other types of smuggling at U.S. ports of entry for the years that were analyzed by CRS. During the four years that were analyzed by CRS, immigration inspectors intercepted more aliens and narcotics being smuggled into the country each year after FY2000 (see Table 2).

Databases

Immigration inspectors use several systems and databases to assist them with identifying aliens who are potentially inadmissible under the INA or otherwise may pose a threat to the country. In particular, four systems are commonly used to screen out individuals:

- Interagency Border Inspections System (IBIS),[193]
- Automated Biometrics Identification System (IDENT),[194]
- National Crime Information System (NCIC III),[195] and
- Passenger Analysis Unit System.[196]

In FY2003, these systems intercepted over 207,000 aliens. In FY2002, over 254,000 aliens were intercepted, an increase of over 66,000 from FY2001.

Selected Immigration Inspections Issues

Since the September 11, 2001, terrorist attacks, considerable concern has been raised because the 19 terrorists were aliens who apparently entered the United States on temporary visas. Although the INA bars terrorists, consular officers issuing the visas and immigration inspectors working at the borders did not have access to *all* the law enforcement and intelligence data that might identify potential terrorists. Congress has enacted major laws requiring information sharing and interoperable databases to screen potential terrorists and criminal aliens, the most recent being the REAL ID Act of 2005.[197] Whether these provisions are being successfully implemented remains an important policy question.[198]

Screening Aliens and Implementation of the US-VISIT Program

While the U.S. Visitor and Immigrant Status Indicator Technology (US-VISIT) program — the automated entry and exit data system that is present at various ports of entry — has been heralded as a tool to enhance border security, critics question whether it will effectively track the entry-exit of suspicious foreign nationals.[199] Some have expressed concern that most Canadians and the 6.4 million Mexicans with border crossing cards are not subjected to the requirements of the US-VISIT program,[200] thus establishing a variety of avenues for potential terrorists and criminals to elude detection through US-VISIT's biometric background checks.

While almost all observers agree that the implementation of US-VISIT has proven to be challenging, especially at land ports of entry, many express confidence that it will ultimately be successful. Administration officials cite the number of aliens apprehended or denied entry as the result of the various systems and databases that comprise US-VISIT as evidence that US-VISIT can achieve its objectives. In 2004, the Administration reported that 100 aliens had "hits" in US-VISIT.[201]

Currently, the US-VISIT program is being implemented at land POEs and therefore only includes a fraction of the total traveling public. According to a DHS Office of Inspector General report published in February 2005, only 2.7% of the traveling public are vetted. The remaining 97.3% are currently exempt from the requirements of the program. To put this in context, of the 97.3% that are not screened through US-VISIT, the plurality (34%) are citizens of the United States, roughly 29% comprise of Mexicans who possess a Laser Visa and 15% are visa-exempt Canadians. Another major category is comprised of Legal Permanent Residents of the United States (which make up 21% of the entering population).

DHS' OIG expressed concern about the number of travelers who are currently exempt from the requirements of the program, including Mexican nationals in possession of a BCC (unless traveling beyond the border zone), and visa-exempt Canadian nationals. Visa-exempt Canadian nationals are exempt from the current travel document requirements,[202] at least until the Western Hemisphere Travel

Initiative is implemented,[203] Mexican nationals in possession of a Laser Visa are also exempt from such requirements.[204]

Biometric Verification System (BVS)

Mexican nationals who plan to stay in the United States for a specified period of time, travel within a certain geographical distance from the border and posseses a Laser Visa are exempt from the requirements of the US-VISIT program. The Administration exempted this category of individuals primarily due to the extensive background check that includes the querying of several criminal and watchlisting databases that is conducted on all Laser Visa applicants. The Administration also contends that the Laser Visa document is read and scanned at the time the Mexican national presents himself for entry to the U.S. at a POE, thus providing an extra layer of security. Observers note, however, that the equipment necessary to read and scan the documents are not at every POE. At POEs where the equipment is being piloted, the equipment is reportedly in the secondary inspections area and does not operate 100% of the time. Moreover, the BVS is not integrated with other critical data systems and databases.

Enforcement Between Ports of Entry[205]

The law prohibits aliens from entering or attempting to enter the United States at any time or place which has not been designated by an immigration officer (i.e., a port of entry). It also prohibits any alien from eluding inspection by immigration officers.[206] The United States Border Patrol (USBP) is tasked with detecting and preventing the entrance of aliens trying to evade inspection by crossing into the United States between ports of entry (POEs). USB's primary mission is to detect and prevent the entry of terrorists, weapons of mass destruction, and unauthorized aliens from coming into the country, and to interdict drug smugglers and other criminals between official ports of entry.

The USBP patrols 8,000 miles of the international borders with Mexico and Canada and the coastal waters around Florida and Puerto Rico.[207] The Southwestern border accounts for over 97% of all illegal alien apprehensions and as a result of this commands the lion's share of USBP resources and manpower. The Northern border, conversely, poses a severe logistical challenge given its length, geography, and comparative lack of manpower.

About 90% of USBP agents are deployed along the Southwest border with Mexico. This deployment reflects the USBP's decade long policy of "Prevention Through Deterrence," which aims to place enough agents and resources directly on the border to deter would-be border crossers and reroute illegal border traffic from traditional urban routes to less populated and geographically harsher areas, providing USBP agents with a tactical advantage over illegal border crossers and smugglers.[208] It also reflects the operational reality that the vast majority of unauthorized migration into the U.S. originates in Mexico.

Shortly after the creation of DHS, the USBP was directed to formulate a new Border Patrol National Strategy that would better reflect the realities of the post 9/11 security landscape. In March of 2005, the USBP unveiled the new strategy, which places greater emphasis on interdicting terrorists and features five main objectives:

- establishing the substantial probability of apprehending terrorists and their weapons as they attempt to enter illegally between the ports of entry;
- deterring illegal entries through improved enforcement;
- detecting, apprehending, and deterring smugglers of humans, drugs, and other contraband;
- leveraging "Smart Border" technology to multiply the deterrent and enforcement effect of agents; and
- reducing crime in border communities, thereby improving the quality of life and economic vitality of those areas.[209]

In the national strategy, DHS notes that while many classify aliens attempting to enter the country illegally between POE as "economic migrants," an "ever present threat exists from the potential for terrorists to employ the same smuggling and transportation networks, infrastructure, drop houses, and other support then use these masses of illegal aliens as 'cover' for a successful cross-border penetration."[210] In an attempt to address this threat, the USBP's new strategy focuses on laying the foundation for achieving operational control over the border. The USBP defines operational control as "the ability to detect, respond to, and interdict border penetrations in areas deemed as high priority for threat potential or other national security objectives."[211] The strategy places greater emphasis on a hierarchical and vertical command structure, featuring a direct chain of command from headquarters to the field.

The strategy also builds on the "Prevention Through Deterrence" strategy outlined in the agency's previous National Strategic Plan by placing added emphasis on enhancing its ability to rapidly deploy agents in response to emerging threats. Tactical, operational, and strategic intelligence is critical to this new emphasis on rapid deployment, as it will allow the USBP to assess risks and target its enforcement efforts to best address those risks. According to the strategy, much of this intelligence will be generated through the use of next generation surveillance systems, including cameras, sensors, and other technologies. Additionally, the USBP will coordinate closely with CBP's Office of Intelligence and other DHS and Federal agencies' intelligence apparatuses. Lastly, the new USBP National Strategy formulates different strategies tailored to each of the agency's three operational theaters: the Southwest border, the Northern border, and the coastal waters around Florida and Puerto Rico.

Apprehensions[212]

The impact of the "Prevention Through Deterrence" strategy has been difficult to gauge. There is considerable evidence that it has made border crossing more challenging, expensive, and dangerous for illegal aliens. However, the total number of aliens apprehended increased steadily from 1994 to 2000 as the number of personnel and resources deployed along the border more than doubled. It is possible that the increased presence of agents and resources stationed on the border led the INS to catch more unauthorized aliens, accounting for the increase in apprehensions. It is also possible that the increase in apprehensions during that period instead reflects an increase in the number of people trying to enter the country in order to benefit from the quickly growing economy of the mid to late 1990s.

Figure 10 shows the recent trends in USBP apprehensions along the border. USBP apprehensions increased steadily through the late 1990s, reaching a peak of 1.68 million in 2000. From 2000 to 2003 apprehensions have declined steadily, reaching a low of 931,557 in 2003. This reduction could be attributed to the "Prevention Through Deterrence" strategy finally reaching a critical mass of enough agents and resources placed directly on the border to severely inhibit illegal migrants from entering the country. Conversely, the reduction may be the result of fewer unauthorized aliens trying to enter the country due to the economic recession and rising unemployment during this period that made finding low paying jobs increasingly difficult for illegal aliens. In addition, the reduction could be an indication that increasing staffing does not increase the USBP's effectiveness. In FY2004, apprehensions increased by 25% to 1.16 million; apprehensions remained relatively stable in FY2005, increasing slightly to 1.2 million.

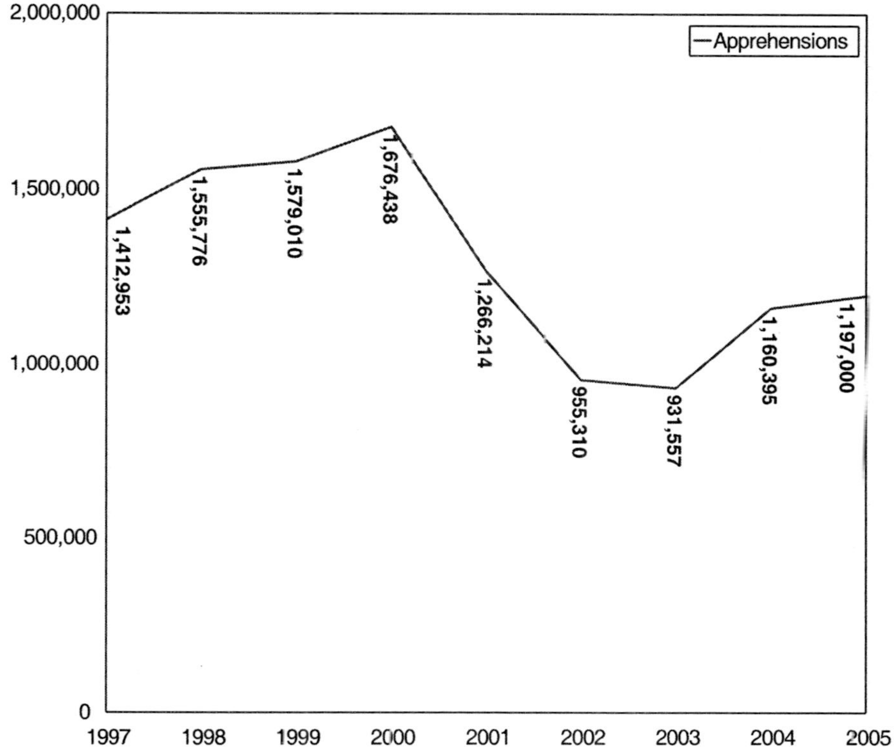

Source: CRS presentation of data from: for 1997, Immigration and Naturalization Service, *FY1997 Statistical Yearbook of the INS*. For FY1998-FY2004, DHS Office of Immigration Statistics, *FY2004 Yearbook of Immigration Statistics*, January 2006. FY2005, DHS, *FY2005 Monthly Statistical Report, Year End*, September 2005.

Figure 10. Border Patrol Apprehensions: FY1997-FY2005.

Enforcement of Immigration Laws and Local Law Enforcement [213]

DHS has a limited number of interior investigators who are charged with enforcing immigration, customs, and other federal law within the interior of the country, compared to over 600,000 state and local law enforcement officers.[214] In an effort to carry out the country's anti-terrorism mission and strengthen the interior enforcement of immigration law, DHS has entered into agreements (Memoranda of Understanding) with several localities that include the deputizing of local law enforcement officers to assist the federal government with enforcing certain aspects of immigration law.[215]

The origins of these agreements date back to 1996. The Illegal Immigration Reform and Immigrant Responsibility Act of 1996 amended the INA by permitting the Attorney General to enter into written agreements with states and localities to allow law enforcement personnel to perform certain immigration functions relating to the investigation, apprehension, or detention of aliens so long as it is consistent with state and local law. The law required that law enforcement personnel performing such functions have knowledge of relevant federal laws and receive adequate training to perform the functions.

Proponents of these agreements argue that the initiative would assist DHS to enforce the immigration law further into the interior of the United States.[216] Also, they assert that the initiative would make it easier to arrest more potential terrorists and foreign born criminals, thus providing an elevated level of security for the nation.[217]

Opponents contend, however, that these agreements undermine the relationship between local law enforcement agencies and the communities they serve,[218] noting that there are existing tensions between local law enforcement agencies and many minority communities, and this tension is heightened when local law enforcement engages in immigration enforcement.[219] For example, potential witnesses and victims of crime may be reluctant to come forward to report crimes in fear of actions that might be taken against them by DHS. They contend that the initiative could result in the reduction of local law enforcement resources as well as the inconsistent application of immigration law across jurisdictions.[220] Some law enforcement officers have raised concerns about the complexities of immigration law creating liability issues.[221]

Resource Allocation

Previously in this report, workload measures were presented for the different types of immigration enforcement activities. For example, for removals, workload was measured in the number of removals, for worksite enforcement in NIFs, for inspectors, the number of inspections. Nonetheless, none of these measures are comparable with each other. For example, comparing the number of inspections with the number of removals does not provide any insight into resource allocation, especially since the staff time devoted to each task is different. It may take three minutes of an inspectors time to process an alien entering the country, where as it may take days or weeks for a special agent to locate and apprehend one illegal alien.

This section examines the *actual hours* spent on different tasks by Special Agents and Immigration Agents from 1992 through 2003. As previously discussed, during 2004, ICE and CBP switched their accounting system from INS' Performance Analysis System (PAS) to the U.S. Customs Service's Treasury Enforcement Communications System (TECS), and as a result, data for 2004 onward are not comparable with previous years. TECS contains fewer data fields than PAS, which means that some of the data in PAS do not exist in TECS. In addition, the data for FY2004 are incomplete in both systems, as the different parts of ICE did not switch from PAS to TECS at the same time.

Interior Enforcement Hours

As discussed above, activities typically label as interior enforcement include the detention and removal of aliens who entered illegally or violated the terms of their admittance, alien smuggling and trafficking investigations, worksite enforcement, and investigations of benefit and document fraud.

Overview

Figure 11 shows that, of the years examined, the number of hours devoted to "interior" enforcement activities was lowest in FY1992 (1,375 workyears).[222] The number of workyears increased slightly between FY1992 and FY1994, and then decreased in FY1995 (1,393 workyears). Between FY1995 and FY1999, the number of workyears increased. Of the years analyzed, the number of workyears reached a peak of 2,081 in FY1999 (the same year that INS released its interior enforcement strategy), declined until FY2002 (1,806), and then increased in FY2003 (1,892).

Between FY1992 and FY2003, the largest number of workyears were devoted to locating and arresting criminal aliens, approximately one-third of all the workyears (see Figure 12). The proportion of workyears related to worksite enforcement has decreased, though not consistently, since FY1992. In FY1992, worksite enforcement accounted for 18.1% of all workyears, whereas in FY2003, worksite enforcement only comprised 3.5% of all workyears. Similarly, the percentage of workyears devoted to fraud investigations was larger in FY1992 (15.3%) than in FY2003 (7.7%). Conversely, the proportion of total hours devoted to status violations and non-investigative work were larger in FY2003 than in FY1992. The percentage of time devoted to smuggling remained relatively stable compared to the trends in the other types of investigations. Notably, in FY2004 and FY2005, ICE suffered funding shortfalls, resulting in training, travel, recruitment, pay, and awards shortages, and as a result it is unlikely that ICE was able to devote additional resources to immigration enforcement during those years.[223]

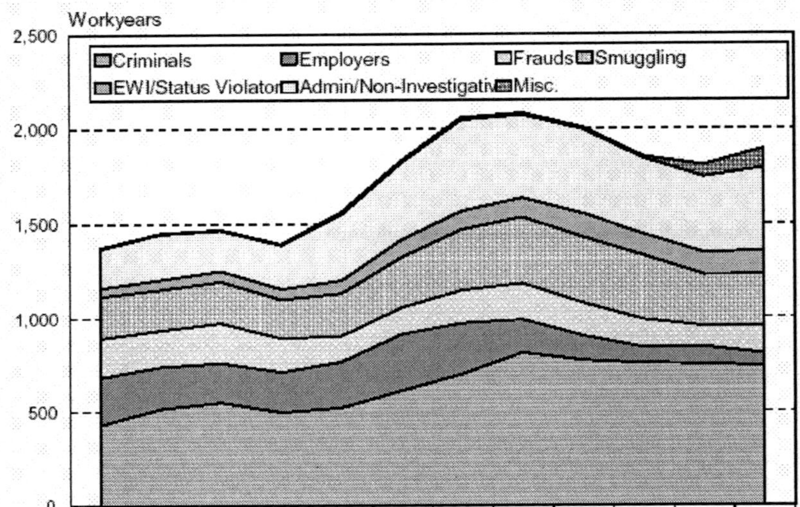

	1992	1993	1994	1995	1996	1997	1998	1999	2000	2001	2002	2003
Total	1,374.1	1,451.4	1,469	1,393.2	1,561.5	1,831.6	2,056.8	2,081	2,005.7	1,851.1	1,806	1,892.1
Misc.	5.5	4.8	3.7	6.7	14	10.9	13.4	10.7	10.7	9.7	62.1	100.6
Admin/Non-Investigative	204.8	239.8	212.9	228.2	345.6	404.5	477.4	437.5	442.4	397.7	398.6	434.9
EWI/Status Violators	45.7	52.1	56.5	57.1	68.5	91.6	98.4	100.5	124.3	111.5	115.6	125.8
Smuggling	225.3	217.9	220.9	211.1	229.5	266.1	318.7	347.5	347.8	344.3	277.2	278.9
Frauds	210.4	199.2	216.1	181.4	140.2	146.9	177.7	194.7	180.8	151.3	110.9	146.1
Employers	249.4	221.1	208.7	210.3	240.3	300	273.2	179.4	129.6	83	90.6	65.6
Criminals	433	516.6	550.2	498.6	523.3	611.6	698	810.7	770.1	753.7	751.1	740.2

Source: CRS analysis of data from DHS' Performance Analysis System (PAS).

Figure 11. Workyears Devoted to Interior Immigration Enforcement Activities by Type: FY1992-FY2003.

Criminal

Historically, the largest proportion of work hours have been devoted to criminal alien cases (see Figures 11 and 12). In FY1992, 433 workyears were spent locating and arresting criminal aliens. That number increased in FY1993 and FY1994 (550), and then decreased in FY1995 (498). Between FY1997 and FY1999, the number of hours devoted to criminal aliens increased, and peaked in FY1999 at 811 workyears. The number of hours devoted to these cases decreased between FY1999 and FY2003. In FY2003, the number of workyears devoted to criminal alien cases was 740, almost double the amount of hours spent on these cases in FY1992.

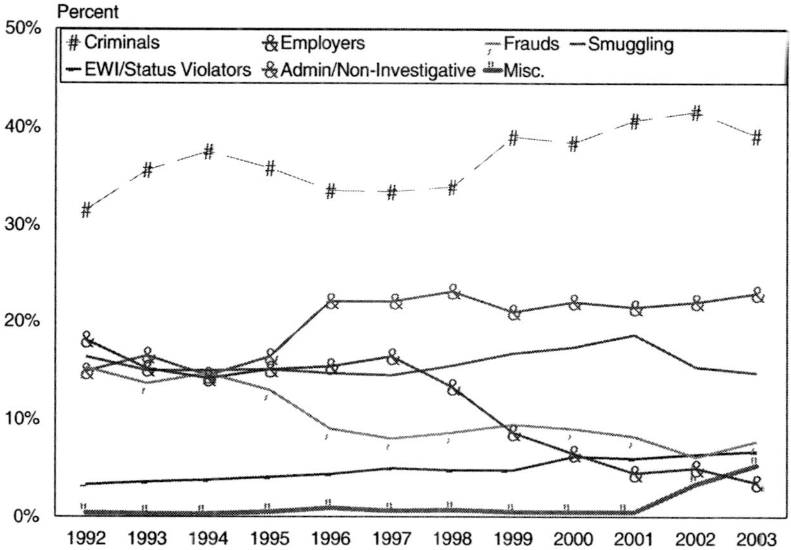

	1992	1993	1994	1995	1996	1997	1998	1999	2000	2001	2002	2003
Criminals	31.5%	35.6%	37.5%	35.8%	33.5%	33.4%	33.9%	39%	38.4%	40.7%	41.6%	39.[illegible]%
Employers	18.1%	15.2%	14.2%	15.1%	15.4%	16.4%	13.3%	8.6%	6.5%	4.5%	5%	3.5%
Frauds	15.3%	13.7%	14.7%	13%	9%	8%	8.6%	9.4%	9%	8.2%	6.1%	7.7%
Smuggling	16.4%	15%	15%	15.1%	14.7%	14.5%	15.5%	16.7%	17.3%	18.6%	15.3%	14.7%
EWI/Status Violators	3.3%	3.6%	3.8%	4.1%	4.4%	5%	4.8%	4.8%	6.2%	6%	6.4%	6.7%
Admin/Non-Investigative	14.9%	16.5%	14.5%	16.4%	22.1%	22.1%	23.2%	21%	22.1%	21.5%	22.1%	23%
Misc.	0.4%	0.3%	0.3%	0.5%	0.9%	0.6%	0.7%	0.5%	0.5%	0.5%	3.4%	5.3%

Source: CRS analysis of data from DHS' Performance Analysis System (PAS).

Figure 12. Percent of Workyears by Enforcement Activity: FY1992-FY2003.

In addition, the increase in actual hours does not correspond to a doubling of the proportion of time spent on criminal alien cases. In FY1992, 31.5% of all hours were spent on criminal alien cases. The proportion of time increased to 37.5% in FY1994, and decreased to 33.4% in FY1997. Between FY1997 and FY2002, the percentage of time devoted to criminal alien cases rose to 41.6% and then decreased to 39.1% in FY2003.

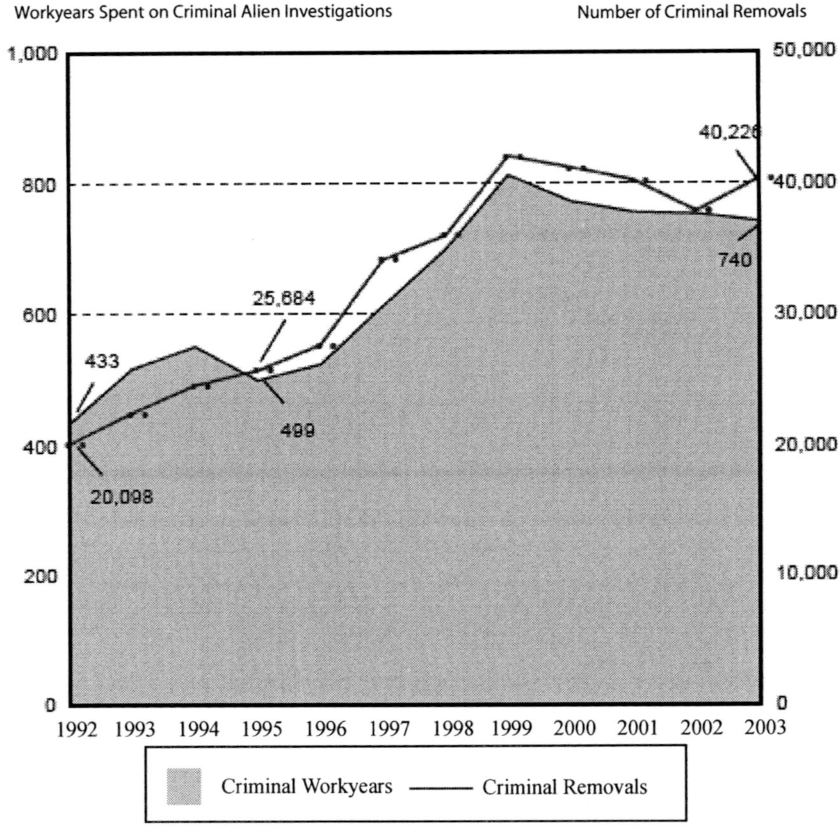

Source: CRS analysis of data from DHS' Performance Analysis System (PAS), and F.Y1992-1997 from Immigration and Naturalization Service, *FY1997 Statistical Yearbook of the INS*. FY1998-FY2004 from DHS Office of Immigration Statistics, *FY2004 Yearbook of Immigration Statistics*, January 2006, p. 162. FY2005, DHS, *FY2005 Monthly Statistical Report, Year End*, September 2005.

Figure 13. Workyears Spent on Criminal Aliens, and Number of Criminal Alien Removals: FY1992-FY2003.

Figure 13 shows that the number of workyears devoted to criminal aliens and the number of criminal alien removals are highly correlated. As the number of workyears devoted to criminal aliens increased, so did the number of aliens removed on criminal grounds. However, from FY2002 to FY2003, the number of hours decreased slightly while the number of criminal removals increased, which may be related to the drop in criminal removals in FY2002. Based on this analysis, one could argue that an increase in resources for criminal alien investigations would result in an increase in removals of criminal aliens. Nonetheless, there may be a limit to the effect that addition of resources will have on criminal alien investigations. For example, an increase in the number of criminal alien arrests would increase the workload of the Executive Office for Immigration Review (EOIR). Thus, if ICE significantly increases their arrests of criminal aliens, the removal cases will still have to be adjudicated by EOIR before the alien can be removed. In addition, since criminal aliens are subject to mandatory detention, increasing the arrests of criminal aliens will increase the need for detention bedspace.

Worksite Enforcement

An analysis of INS investigation workload data reveals that time spent on employer cases by agents, supervisors, and non-clerical support personnel accounted for less than 18% of total investigation workyears in each year from FY1992 through FY2003 (See Figures 11 and 12). One factor routinely cited to explain why a greater share of interior enforcement resources was not available for employer cases is the growth of the criminal alien workload in the 1990s.[224] According to Under Secretary Hutchinson, the criminal alien workload "eventually grew to the point that it consumed more investigative hours than any other enforcement activity."[225]

Figures 11 and 12 reflect a series of changes to the worksite enforcement program that occurred over the FY1992-FY2003 period. During the first half of this period, as Figures 11 and 12 show, time spent on worksite enforcement, both in terms of number of workyears and as a percentage of total investigations workyears, decreased until FY1994 and then began increasing. The mid-1990s increase coincided with actions by the Clinton Administration and Congress to bolster worksite enforcement.

After FY1997, as Figures 11 and 12 show, time spent on employer cases trended downward. In FY2003, worksite enforcement accounted for 3.5% of the total investigation workyears, less than one-fifth of its share in FY1992. The start of this decline coincided with a change in INS's approach to worksite enforcement, set forth in a May 1998 memorandum by INS Executive Associate Commissioner for Field Operations Michael Pearson.[226] Apparently, the change was prompted largely by complaints about INS tactics during worksite raids. According to Pearson, the new procedures described in the memorandum and the accompanying materials responded to complaints by Congress and others, and incorporated the "best practices" of various offices.[227]

Fraud

As Figures 11 and 12 illustrate, fraud investigations have declined from FY1992 through FY2003, both as percent of interior enforcement and in terms of actual workyears. Although there appears to be an upturn, most likely due to the 1999 Interior Enforcement Strategy mentioned previously, the overall trends have been downward. As a percent of interior enforcement workyears, fraud investigations dropped from 15.3% in FY1992 to 7.7% in FY2003. Actual workyears fell from 210 to 146 over the same period.

Smuggling

For the years analyzed, the peak workyears and the largest percentage of all interior enforcement hours devoted to alien smuggling correspond to the first three years of the INS interior enforcement strategy (FY1999 through FY2001) when alien smuggling was the agency's second highest priority. (The removal of criminal aliens was the first priority.) After FY2001, the number of workyears as well as the percentage of all hours devoted to alien smuggling declined, possibly as a result of shifting priorities after the terrorist attacks in September 2001. The number of hours devoted to smuggling cases was the lowest in FY1995 (211 workyears), and largest in FY1999 and FY2000 (348 workyears). The proportion of all interior enforcement hours devoted to alien smuggling was smallest in FY1997 (14.5%), and largest in FY2001 (18.6%). In FY2003, 279 workyears were devoted to smuggling cases which corresponded to 14.7% of all interior enforcement workyears. Nonetheless, according to ICE the resources and time devoted to alien smuggling are larger if other relevant investigative programs (such as criminal aliens, identity and benefit fraud, and the Joint Terrorism Task Force) are included in the total.[228] (See Figures 11 and 12.)

Status Violators

Status violators are aliens who have entered without inspection or have overstayed their visas (i.e., the alien is out of status). As shown in Figure 11, the number of hours spent on status violators almost tripled between FY1992 and FY2000, from 46 workyears to 124 workyears. The percentage of overall investigative time spent on status violation investigations doubled during that time period, as did the resident unauthorized alien population in the United States.[229]

(See Figure 12.) In FY1992, 3.3% of all hours were devoted to status violations compared to 6.7% of all hours in FY2003. The number of hours spent on status violators, as well as the percent of time devoted to status violators, declined between FY2000 and FY2001, then increased between FY2001 and FY2003. Nonetheless, it is interesting to note, that in the most recent data year, only 6.7% of investigative hours were spend on status violators when the unauthorized population was estimated to be almost 10 million.

Administrative and Other

The amount of hours spent on administrative and non-investigative tasks more than doubled between FY1992 and FY1998, from 205 workyears to 477 workyears, as illustrated in Figure 11. Similarly, as shown in Figure 12, the percent of hours devoted to administrative tasks increased from 14.9% to 23.2%, the largest proportion devoted to administrative duties for any year. It is interesting to note that in 1999, INS released its interior enforcement strategy which may account for the increase in non-investigative hours. In addition, the increase in administrative and other hours may be the result of an increase in time devoted to developing databases, including the development of an entry/exit system which was mandated in IIRIRA in 1996.

In FY2003, 23% of all hours (435 workyears) were devoted to administrative and non-investigative tasks. In addition, the percent of time devoted to miscellaneous tasks remained under 1% until FY2002 and FY2003, and then increased in both years. (See Figure 12.) This increase may be attributable to the productivity time lost/needed when DHS was being formed.

Border Enforcement

Inspectors

As Figure 9 and Table 2 above shows, the number of hours spent on inspection duties increased between FY1992 (2,273 workyears) and FY1994 (2,446 workyears), decreased in FY1995 (2,245 workyears), and then steadily increased until FY2000 (3,189 workyears). The total number of hours decreased between FY2000 and FY2001, increased between FY2001 and FY2002, and then decreased to the lowest level of the period in FY2003 (2,098 workyears).

The largest percentage of hours for inspectors is spent in primary inspections, and this proportion has been fairly constant through the years analyzed, ranging from 62.2% (FY1998) to 69.8% (FY2001). In FY2003, immigration inspectors spent 13% of their time on enforcement-related activities.[230] Over the previous 11 years, the time spent by immigration inspectors on enforcement activities has steadily risen, with the exceptions of FY1996 when the percentage dropped by one percent from FY1995, and FY2001 when the percentage dropped by three percent from FY2000. (See Figure 9 and Table 2.)

USBP

The number of hours worked by the USBP, mostly spent patrolling the border between points of entry, almost doubled between FY1997 and FY2002, from

3,073 workyears to 6,096 workyears (See Figure 14). The number of USBP workyears decreased slightly, by three workyears between FY2002 and FY2003. The workyears for USBP increased dramatically between FY2003 and FY2005. In FY2004, USBP spent 6,591 workyears on enforcement efforts, and in FY2005, 8,018 workyears.

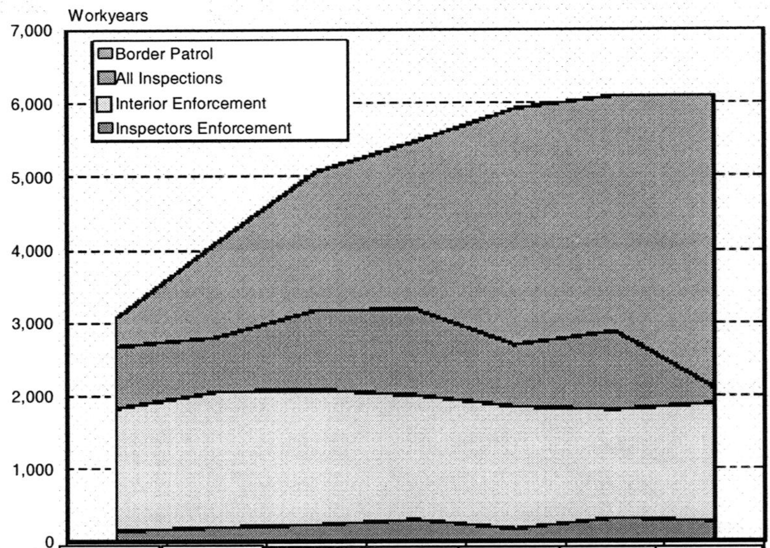

	1997	1998	1999	2000	2001	2002	2003
Border Patrol	3,072.7	4,099.5	5,069	5,478.3	5,923.2	6,095.9	6,093
All inspections	2,664.0	2,795.9	3,173.7	3,188.6	2,683.5	2,871.6	2,098
Interior Enforcement	1,831.6	2,056.8	2,081	2,005.7	1,851.1	1,806	1,892.1
Inspectors Enforcement	140.9	190.9	224.6	294.3	164.5	315.8	270.7

Source: CRS analysis of data from the Performance Analysis System (PAS).

Figure 14. USBP, Inspectors, and Interior Enforcement Workyears: FY1997-FY2003.

Interestingly, as illustrated in Figure 15, an increase in workyears does not automatically result in an increase in apprehensions. Between FY1997 and FY2000, both workyears and apprehensions increased. In FY2001 and FY2002, although USBP workyears continued to increase, the number of apprehensions decreased. Between FY2003 and FY2004, the workyears increased eight percent from 6,093 to 6,591, while apprehensions increased 25% from 931,557 to 1.2 million. Comparatively, between FY2004 and FY2005, the number of USBP workyears increased 22% from 6,591 to 8,018, while the number of apprehensions increased only 3%. The decrease in apprehensions since FY2000 may be attributable to fewer unauthorized aliens trying to enter the country due to the economic recession, and the increased difficulty finding employment. USBP argues that the reason why apprehensions do not seem to be increasing at the same rate as resources is because the “Prevention through Deterrence” strategy is finally reaching a critical mass of enough agents and resources placed directly on the border to severely inhibit illegal migrants from entering the country.[231] It may be that additional agents do not have a large effect on apprehensions, or that the additional number of agents is not large enough to actually increase apprehensions.

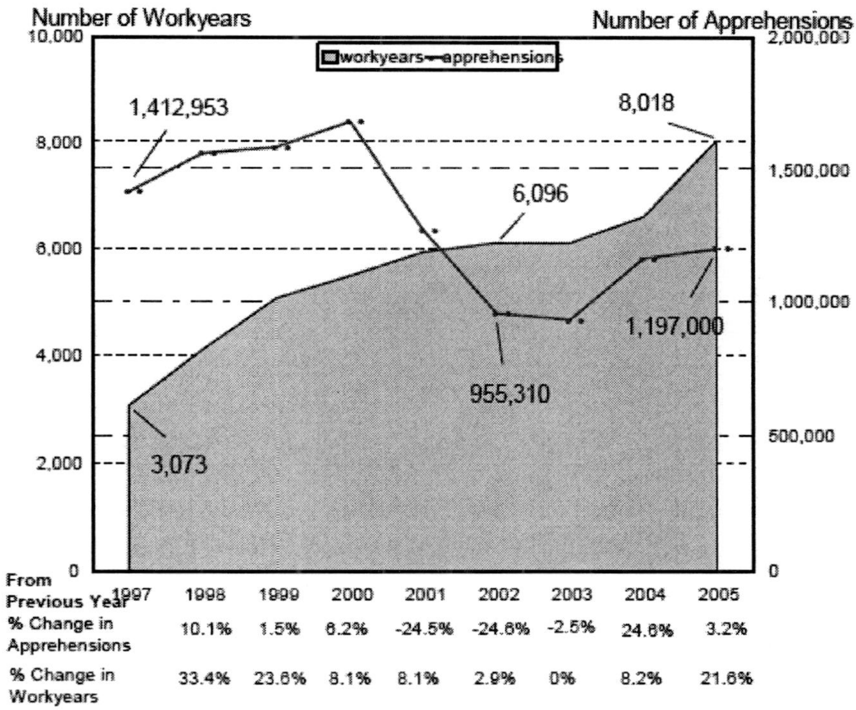

Source: CRS analysis of unpublished DHS data; CRS presentation of data from the following sources: for 1997, Immigration and Naturalization Service, FY1997 Statistical Yearbook of the INS. For FY1998-FY2004, DHS Office of Immigration Statistics, FY2004 Yearbook of Immigration Statistics, January 2006. FY2005, DHS, FY2005 Monthly Statistical Report, Year End, September 2005.

Figure 15. Border Patrol: Apprehension, Workyears, and Percent Change, FY1997-FY2005

Comparison

Figure 14 illustrates that many more resources (measured in staff hours) have been allotted to enforcement between the ports of entry than enforcement within the United States and at the ports of entry. While the amount of USBP resources significantly increased between FY1997 and FY2003, the resources for both inspections and interior enforcement increased more modestly between FY1997 and FY1999, while inspection hours also increased between FY1999 and FY2000. Hours for interior enforcement, saw a mix of increases and decreased during that period. Between FY2000 and FY2002 interior enforcement hours decreased, and then increased between FY2002 and FY2003. Nonetheless, for the years analyzed, workyears spent on interior enforcement were highest in FY1999, the first year of the INS' interior enforcement strategy. Inspection hours decreased between FY2000 and FY2001, increased in FY2002, and then decreased again in FY2003. The amount of time inspectors spend on enforcement activities, increased between FY1997 and FY2000, decreased substantially in FY2001, and then increased substantially in FY2002. Between FY2002 and FY2003, the number of inspector enforcement hours decreased.

Comparing FY1997 with FY2003, the USBP hours almost doubled from 3,073 to 6,093 workyears, while the interior enforcement hours increased slightly from 1,832 to 1,892 workyears, and the number of inspection hours fell from 2,665 to 2,098. Nonetheless, a comparison of FY1997 and FY2003, shows that amount of time inspectors spent on enforcement activities almost doubled, from 141 workyears to 271 workyears. Importantly, inspection hours are dependent on workload, (i.e., how many people are entering the country in any one year), but since the number of aliens illegally present in the country continues to grow, it is difficult to argue that there has been a decrease in the interior or border enforcement workload.

DHS Organizational Structure

Questions have been raised concerning the impact of DHS's organizational structure on the effective enforcement of immigration laws.[232] Nonetheless, any attempt to determine the consequence of DHS's structure on immigration enforcement, involves disentangling (1) issues that remain from the former INS (i.e., are the problems encountered by ICE and CBP the same as those found in the former INS); (2) issues related to the time needed for a newly created department to function smoothly; and (3) issues related to the separation of immigration enforcement functions into separate agencies — especially the distinction between CBP and ICE. Although this section focuses on some of the issues facing the new department, it is important to note that there are benefits to combining the disparate agencies in the new department.. For example, ICE can pursue money laundering charges related to smuggling and document fraud through the Financial Investigations Division. This capacity did not exist in INS, and INS would have had to seek outside assistance to pursue additional charges.[233]

Inherited INS Issues

Over the years, GAO completed several reports on the management in the former INS which noted that INS faced significant challenges in assembling the basic systems and processes that organizations need to complete their goal.[234] GAO found a lack of

- clearly delineated roles and responsibilities leading to overlapping responsibilities and ineffective use of resources (e.g., lacking the ability to determine staffing needs);
- policies and procedures to balance competing priorities such as working level guidance;[235]
- effective internal and external communication and coordination (i.e, a lack of clarity on responsibilities and authorities); and
- automated systems to provide accurate and timely information to support its operations.

In testimony before the House Judiciary Committee, Subcommittee on Immigration, Border Security, and Claims in April 2003, GAO noted that "unless these elements were established, enforcing immigration laws..., and effectively participating in the government wide efforts to combat terrorism would be problematic regardless of how the immigration function was organized."[236]

INS faced numerous challenges implementing its interior enforcement strategy.[237] Historically, Congress and INS devoted five times more resources (staff and funding) to border enforcement than to interior enforcement.[238] The INS claimedthat it lacked sufficient staff to reach its interior enforcement goals, but the agency never performed a systematic assessment of their staffing needs to reach program goals and the best allocation of existing staff resources.[239] GAO testified in 2003 that the challenges in the Interior Enforcement program would require high-level attention and a concerted effort from ICE. For example, there were hundreds of thousands of criminal aliens, the number of aliens smuggled into the United States had grown along with the complexity of the alien smuggling operations, tens of thousands of aliens illegally seek to gain immigration benefit, and millions of unauthorized aliens use fraudulent documents to gain employment.[240]

In a 2004 report, GAO found that DHS management issues were similar to those in the former INS. For example, as in the former INS, DHS lacks clarity and formal guidelines for addressing overlapping roles and responsibilities of ICE and CBP, which has lead to disagreements, confusion, and institutional barriers between the two agencies.[241]

Database Integration

INS had a longstanding history of using antiquated databases and in some cases had paper-based systems. Several GAO reports and one by the DOJ Inspector General noted the outdated systems and databases that immigration officials used to conduct their daily business.[242] Prompted by the 2001 terrorist attacks, in 2002 Congress passed the Enhanced Border Security and Visa Entry Reform Act of 2002.[243] The act mandated the integration of immigration data systems and databases. The act also called for the integration of data systems and databases that contain federal law enforcement and intelligence information relevant to making decisions on visa admissibility and the removal of aliens.

Many assert that the need for all agencies involved in admitting aliens to share intelligence and coordinate activities is essential for U.S. immigration policy to be effective in securing the homeland. Some maintain that the reforms Congress made in the mid-1990s requiring all visa applicants to be checked against lookout databases were inadequate because the databases across the relevant agencies were not interoperable and the various agencies were territorial with their data. They maintain that, in the long run, the most efficient and effective guard against the entry of aliens who would do us harm is an interagency and inter-departmental database that is accessible in "real time" to consular officers, CBP inspectors, and key law enforcement and intelligence officials.

Others point to the cost, time, and complexity of developing interoperable databases. They cite the difficulty thus far in determining what biometric identifiers are most appropriate for screening aliens.[244] They point out competing technologies of the existing databases in which various key agencies have already heavily invested. Some maintain that success of the interoperable database technology depends on 100% inclusion of aliens applying for visas and seeking admission, but that the sheer scope of such a system poses "real time" implementation issues. They also warn that if intelligence data becomes too accessible across agencies, national security may actually be breached because sensitive information may be more likely to fall into the wrong hands. Privacy concerns arise as well as the data sharing and interoperability broadens.

Separation of Immigration Functions Into Separate DHS Agencies

When ICE and CBP were created, neither agency was given responsibility for all immigration enforcement activities, and neither was designated the lead agency in immigration enforcement. ICE received INS' investigations and intelligence functions, as well as its detention and removal. CBP received the inspections functions and the border patrol. CBP and ICE need to heavily rely on each other because within the new structure, enforcement efforts initiated by CBP often are supposed to be completed by ICE. In addition, CBP border patrol agents are dependent on ICE's DRO for the detention and removal of some of the aliens that they apprehend.[245] Nonetheless, there have been reports of rivalries between ICE and CBP, which inhibit coordination. Moreover, the creation of the DHS has meant that in order to implement an interior enforcement strategy, ICE has to coordinate with CBP and Bureau of Citizenship and Immigration Services (USCIS).[246] As discussed above, when the Department of Homeland Security was formed, USCIS was tasked with the adjudication (service) functions of the former INS.

INS and U.S. Customs Service investigators and intelligence analysts were merged into ICE's investigations and intelligence offices, and INS' detention and removal program was placed in ICE's detention and removal office (DRO). Traditionally, INS investigators specialized in immigration enforcement (e.g., locating criminal aliens, alien smuggling) while Customs investigators specialized in customs enforcement (e.g., drug smuggling, money laundering). In addition, INS investigators primarily investigated civil violations of immigration law, while customs investigators investigated criminal violations related to Customs law. INS and Customs investigators brought their own cultures, policies, mission priorities, procedures to the newly created ICE, which is the second largest investigative bureau in the federal government with approximately 20,000 employees.[247] Conversely, CBP blended entities with similar missions.

Although much of the Congressional attention has focused on the division of ICE and CBP, some issues have also been raised concerning the interaction between USCIS and ICE. INS' approach to benefit fraud was fragmented and unfocused. INS also failed to establish guidance to assure that high-priority cases were investigated.[248] With the creation of DHS, investigating benefit fraud became the responsibility of ICE. Nonetheless, ICE reportedly did not do this, and USCIS established its own benefits fraud investigations unit. According to ICE, it only handles cases of large and expansive benefit fraud which are referred to them from USCIS. All other cases of benefit fraud are handled by USCIS.[249]

OIG Merger Report

DHS' Office of the Inspector General (OIG) examined the merits of merging CBP and ICE, in a report based largely on testimonial evidence. The OIG analyzed whether the difficulties encountered were due to the implementation of the new department or to inherited pre-existing conditions from the former INS. The report also considered other factors such as funding problems and accounting system difficulties. The OIG concluded that organizational structure at the time[250] contributed to the problems in three major areas: (1) coordination between apprehensions and detention and removal efforts, (2) coordination between interdiction and investigative efforts, and (3) coordination of intelligence activities.[251]

The report found that the role of integrating ICE and CBP activities had been the responsibility of Directorate of Border of Transportation Security (BTS) which oversaw both ICE and CBP, but due to staffing shortfalls and a lack of authority (including budget authority) over the bureaus, BTS failed to: (1) prevent ICE and CBP from working at cross purposes; (2) synchronize CBP and ICE operations; and (3) resolve conflicts between the two agencies. The report concluded that CBP and ICE had failed to coordinate efforts, and that each organization engaged in discrete planning and strategy development processes (leading to different priorities), and field staff were accountable to separate chains of command. In addition, the report indicated that the division between ICE and CBP is marked by a clear institutional barrier, and the shortfalls in operational coordination and information sharing have fostered negative relations between CBP and ICE personnel, including competition and mistrust.[252]

Many have said that a merger the magnitude of DHS would take five years or more to settle into satisfactory operations; however, the OIG concluded that the integration has not progressed as well as expected, noting that the people they interviewed almost universally stated that the current problems were seen as unresolvable because of the "unnatural separation" of interdependent functions.[253] Nonetheless, DHS responded to the OIG's recommendation to merge ICE and CBP by maintaining another reorganization would entail costs, including loss of employee productivity during the transition. In addition, DHS noted that the new organization could be too big and unwieldy, with an overly large span of control. Moreover, the report indicated that other agencies may fear that a combined border security agency would become the dominant law enforcement entity.[254]

Furthermore, the Secretary of Homeland Security, Michael Chertoff, undertook a review of the department (called the Second Stage Review) and after careful study concluded that the best course was not to merge ICE and CBP, but to institute a new management structure to reduce bureaucracy, improve accountability, and enhance coordination. Secretary Chertoff also concluded that a merger would diminish the roles of the Assistant Secretary of ICE and the Commissioner of CBP, creating a new bureaucratic reporting mechanism which would diminish coordination rather than enhance it. Secretary Chertoff recommended innovation rather than another massive reorganization.[255]

Investigations

The OIG concluded that the current organizational structure has also hampered coordination of interdiction and investigative efforts. Since the investigative functions have been separated into ICE, CBP officers have reported that ICE no longer accepts as many case referrals from CBP inspectors and border patrol agents. ICE reported that investigative coordination is declining because CBP increasingly refers cases to other agencies such as the FBI and DEA without notifying ICE. In addition, ICE has reported that investigations have been compromised due to CBP's "inexperienced" investigative work.[256] Reportedly, CBP is now developing its own investigative capabilities. Nonetheless, CBP and ICE managers have asserted that the policy is to refer all cases to ICE for investigation.[257]

Intelligence

With the formation of DHS, all immigration intelligence agents including those from the border patrol were placed in ICE's intelligence program, which is responsible for collecting, analyzing, and disseminating immigration related intelligence used by ICE, CBP and USCIS.[258] However, CBP recently established its own intelligence program. CBP and ICE intelligence requirements overlap to a large extent, but the two bureaus have separate intelligence structures and products. The OIG reported that the intelligence coordination needs to improve, and that the only significant coordination between ICE and CBP relates to intelligence received from other agencies.[259]

The organization's primary means of sharing intelligence is through the Treasury Enforcement Communications System (TECS) which was not designed for this purpose as it does not highlight trends or detect anomalies. In addition, most CBP personnel lack the required clearance to retrieve critical information entered into TECS by ICE. The OIG concluded that the reliance on the system is inhibiting the timely and effective exchange of information.[260]

CONCLUSION

Many duties are incorporated under the banner of immigration enforcement. These include removing aliens who should not be in the United States, investigating alien smuggling and trafficking, patrolling between and at ports of entry, combating document and benefit fraud, and enforcing the prohibitions against employers hiring aliens without work authorization. Due to the breadth of immigration enforcement activities, the allocation of resources appears to be significant in determining the ability to enforce the immigration laws. Nonetheless, some contend a policy based solely on enforcement is bound to fail, and only a legalization program, providing a clean slate, can reduce the unauthorized population.[261] However, others assert that the United States has not tried immigration enforcement, arguing that most of the resources have been devoted to border enforcement, and that the United States has not fully engaged in other types of immigration enforcement, most notably worksite enforcement.[262]

The majority of aliens come to the United States for economic opportunities and for family reunification. The ability to contain illegal migration caused by those seeking family reunification may also depend on the ability of DHS to clear the backlog of immigration petitions, and process new petitions. In addition, the per-country ceilings on certain types of family based immigration affect the ability of aliens from countries with high levels of immigration (e.g., the Philippines) to immigrate.[263] Congressional action would be needed to change the per-country ceilings.[264] Some maintain that only reform of the legal immigration system can decrease illegal immigration.[265]

In addition, the amount of illegal migration may also be dependent on the economic health of the sending countries, especially of those countries in the Americas. Factors in other countries effect the desire of their populations to immigrate, legally or illegally, to the United States. For example, between 2000 and 2003, Uruguay experienced a recession increasing the propensity of its citizens to live and work illegally in the United States.[266] Thus, some argue that only a guest worker program, creating opportunities for a large number of immigrants to come to the United States to work, could significantly reduce the unauthorized migration.[267] However, others argue that better worksite enforcement and enforcement document fraud would make it more difficult for unauthorized aliens to find work, resulting in a decrease in the unauthorized population.[268] It is possible that a combination of a guest worker program and increased worksite enforcement may be utilized to reduce the unauthorized population.

Although within the United States, the enforcement of immigration law is primarily the responsibility of the Department of Homeland Security's Bureaus of Immigration and Customs Enforcement (ICE) and Customs and Border Protection (CBP), one possible option to aid in the reduction of the unauthorized alien population might be to increase the coordination and information sharing with other federal agencies, such as the Social Security Administration and the Department of Labor. Another approach may be to increase the role of local law enforcement agencies in the enforcement of immigration laws.[269] Yet many fear that these options will distract the agencies from their primary missions and could hinder the agencies ability to perform other functions if unauthorized aliens will not interact with them.

In some instances, the enforcement of certain immigration laws can be controversial. Although few would argue that aliens should be allowed to enter without being inspected by an immigration officer, and that smugglers and traffickers should not be punished, enforcement against longer-term, noncriminal, unauthorized aliens is often politically difficult due to these aliens' long standing ties to their communities. Often these aliens are integrated in their communities, and the government's attempts to remove them can result in a backlash from the community. Furthermore, there are concerns that increased enforcement against aliens working illegally will disrupt sectors of the economy that depend on foreign labor, and harm the United States economy. The conflicting pressures to reduce the unauthorized population while safeguarding the U.S. economy and maintaining good will among the populace, as well as resource constraints and management issues in DHS, combine to make immigration enforcement policy a complex issue.

APPENDIX A: LIST OF ACRONYMS

BIA	Board of Immigration Appeals (in the Executive Office for Immigration Review)
CBP	Bureau of Customs and Border Protections (in the Department of Homeland Security)
DHS	Department of Homeland Security
DOJ	Department of Justice

DOS	Department of State
DRO	Office of Detention and Removal (in the Bureau of Immigration and Customs Enforcement)
EOIR	Executive Office for Immigration Review (in the Department of Justice)
ESA	Employment Standards Administration (in the Department of Labor)
ICE	Bureau of Immigration and Customs Enforcement (in the Department of Homeland Security)
IJ	Immigration Judge (works in Executive Office for Immigration Review)
INA	Immigration and Nationality Act (Title 8 of the United States Code)
OI	Office of Investigations (in the Bureau of Immigration and Customs Enforcement)
OR	Own Recognizance
NIT	Notice of Intent to Fine
NTA	Notice to Appear
POE	Port of entry
SSA	The Social Security Administration
SSN	Social Security Number
USBP	United States Border Patrol (in the Bureau of Customs and Border Protections)
USCIS	Bureau of Citizenship and Immigration Services (in the Department of Homeland Security)

REFERENCES

[1] An *alien* is "any person not a citizen or national of the United States" and is synonymous with *noncitizen.*

[2] Jeffrey S. Passel, *Unauthorized Migrants: Numbers and Characteristics*, Pew Hispanic Center, June 14, 2005, at [http://www.pewhispanic.org].

[3] Department of Homeland Security, Bureau of Customs and Border Protection, "National Border Patrol Strategy," March 1, 2005, p. 5; and Marc Cooper, "Dead in Their Tracks," *LA Weekly*, Feb. 24, 2006, p. 32.

[4] Testimony of Executive Director of the Center of Immigration Studies, Mark Krikorian, in U.S. Congress House Judiciary Committee, Subcommittee on Immigration, Border Security, and Claims, *Department of*

Homeland Security Transition: Bureau of Immigration and Customs Enforcement, hearings, 108th Cong., 1st sess., Apr. 10, 2003. (Hereafter cited as Krikorian, *Department of Homeland Security Transition: Bureau of Immigration and Customs Enforcement.*)

[5] Ibid.

[6] Steven A. Camarota, *The Open Door: How Militant Islamic Terrorists Entered and Remained in the United States,* (Washington: Center for Immigration Studies, May 2002).

[7] Belinda I. Reyes, Hans P. Johnson, and Richard Van Swearingen, *Holding the Line? The Effect of Recent Border Build-up on Unauthorized Immigration,* Public Policy Institute of California, July 2002, p. 80. (Hereafter cited as Reyes, *Holding the Line? The Effect of Recent Border Build-up on Unauthorized Immigration.*)

[8] Importantly, the discussions of certain enforcement activities (e.g., worksite enforcement and alien smuggling) are more detailed than those for other activities since CRS does not have individual reports on these subjects.

[9] For example, this includes an alien who overstays his visa or an alien who is working when his visa prohibits employment.

[10] Department of Homeland Security, *Securing our Homeland: The U.S. Department of Homeland Security Strategic Plan,* 2004. At [http://www.dhs.gov/interweb/assetlibrary/DHS_StratPlan_FINAL_spread.pdf].

[11] The Homeland Security Act of 2002 (P.L. 107-296) abolished the INS and transferred most of its functions to various bureaus in the new Department of Homeland Security (DHS) effective Mar. 1, 2003.

[12] As quoted by Representative George Gekas in U.S. Congress, House Judiciary Committee, Subcommittee on Immigration and Claims, *INS Interior Enforcement,* hearings, 107th Cong., 2nd sess., June 19, 2002.

[13] Steven A. Camarota, *The Open Door: How Militant Islamic Terrorists Entered and Remained in the United States* (Washington: Center for Immigration Studies, May 2002).

[14] This section adapted from CRS Report RL32270, *Enforcing Immigration Law: The Role of State and Local Law Enforcement,* by Lisa M. Seghetti, Steven R. Vina, and Karma Ester.

[15] Codified as amended at 8 U.S.C. §§1101 *et seq.*

[16] Codified as amended at 8 U.S.C. §§1357 and 1225. The combination or cross-designation of inspectors from Customs, the INS, and the U.S. Department of Agriculture within DHS's Bureau of Customs and Border

Protection, however, may allow the use of other enforcement authorities depending on the circumstance.

[17] References to the Attorney General or the Commissioner of the former INS are now deemed to refer to the Secretary of DHS or his delegates. See P.L. 107-296, §§102(a), 441, 1512(d), and 1571; 8 C.F.R. §2.1, §103.1.

[18] 8 C.F.R. §287.5.

[19] For more discussion of the USA PATRIOT Act and the Enhanced Border Security and Visa Reform Act, see CRS Report RS21438, *Immigration Legislation Enacted in the 107th Congress*, by Andorra Bruno.

[20] See CRS Report RL31560, *Homeland Security Proposals: Issues Regarding Transfer of Immigration Agencies and Functions*, by Lisa M. Seghetti and Ruth Ellen Wasem.

[21] For a detailed discussion of National Intelligence Reform Act, see CRS Report RL32616, *9/11 Commission: Legislative Action Concerning U.S. Immigration Law and Policy in the 108th Congress*, by Michael John Garcia and Ruth Ellen Wasem.

[22] For more discussion of the REAL ID Act, see CRS Report RL33125, *Immigration Legislation and Issues in the 109th Congress*, coordinated by Andorra Bruno.

[23] DHS, *An Assessment of the Proposal to Merge Customs and Border Protection with Immigration and Customs Enforcement*, p. 18.

[24] Ibid., p. 41.

[25] Government Accountability Office, *Immigration Enforcement: DHS Has Incorporated Immigration Enforcement Objectives and Is Addressing Future Planning Requirements,* Oct. 2004 (GAO-05-66), p. 2. (Hereafter cited as GAO, *Immigration Enforcement: DHS Has Incorporated Immigration Enforcement Objectives and Is Addressing Future Planning Requirements*.)

[26] Ibid., p. 2.

[27] Alien smuggling and trafficking is addressed by the human trafficking unit within OI's Smuggling and Public Safety Investigations Division. Community complaints about illegal immigration are addressed by the human trafficking unit and the human rights unit within the Smuggling and Public Safety Investigations Division. Benefit and document fraud is addressed by the identity and benefit fraud unit in the Smuggling and Public Safety Investigations Division, and the visa security unit in the International Affairs Division. USCIS also has its own benefit fraud unit. Worksite enforcement particularly as it pertains to critical infrastructure (e.g.,

airports, power plants) is conducted by the critical infrastructure protection unit in the National Security Investigations Division.

[28] GAO, *Immigration Enforcement: DHS Has Incorporated Immigration Enforcement Objectives and Is Addressing Future Planning Requirements*, p. 2.

[29] See CRS Report RL32562, *Border Security: The Role of the U.S. Border Patrol*, by Blas Nuñez-Neto; and RL32399, *Border Security: Inspections Practices, Policies, and Issues*, coordinated by Ruth Ellen Wasem.

[30] Recently, DHS has begun the Secure Border Initiative (SBI), a multi-year plan which includes increasing USBP agents, expanding detention and removal capabilities, upgrading the technology used at the border, improving the border infrastructure, and increasing interior enforcement. For more information on the SBI see [http://www.cbp.gov/xp/cgov/newsroom/fact_sheets/border/secure_border_initiative/sec ure_border.xml], last visited on March 31, 2006.

[31] For example, see Wayne A. Cornelius, "Death at the Border: Efficacy and Unintended Consequences of US Immigration Control Policy," *Population and Development Review*, vol. 27, no. 4 (Dec. 2001), p. 666.

[32] The following paragraph is adapted from CRS Report RL32270, *Enforcing Immigration Law: The Role of State and Local Law Enforcement*, by Lisa M. Seghetti, Steven R. Vina, and Karma Ester.

[33] INA §237(a)(1)(B). Other examples of civil violations include §243(c) (penalties relating to vessels and aircraft) and §274D (penalties for failure to depart).

[34] Other criminal provisions include §243(a) disobeying a removal order, §1306 offenses relating to registration of aliens, and §274A(f) engaging in a pattern or practice of hiring illegal aliens.

[35] An alien may be present in the United States but not admitted. For example, if an alien entered the United States without being inspected by an immigration officer, the alien would be physically present in the United States, but would not have been admitted under the law.

[36] All aliens must satisfy to DHS inspectors upon entry to the United States that they are not ineligible for admission under the so-called "grounds for inadmissibility" of INA §212. These include health-related grounds, criminal history, national security and terrorist concerns, becoming a public charge, seeking to work without proper labor certification, illegal entry and immigration law violations, lack of proper documents, ineligibility for citizenship, and aliens previously removed.

[37] Moral turpitude is not easily defined under immigration law. Some argue that the flexibility in the term allows for changing social norms.

[38] The definition of aggravated felony (defined in INA §101(a)(43)) includes over 50 types of crimes. In addition, an alien convicted of an aggravated felony is conclusively presumed to be deportable (INA §238(c)). Misdemeanors at the state level may be aggravated felonies under the INA.

[39] So few aliens have been deported under these grounds since 1980, that DHS does not report the number.

[40] 8 C.F.R. §239.1(a)

[41] There is a five-year bar to admissibility for aliens who have been subjected to expedited removal or those ordered removed when trying to enter the United States. There is a 10-year bar for admission for those who were ordered deported. There is a 20-year bar for those who have been previously removed, and those convicted of an aggravated felony are permanently inadmissible. INA §212(a)(9)(A).

[42] Charles Gordon, Stanley Mailman, Stephen Yale-Loehr, *Immigration Law and Procedure.* Newark: LexisNexis, vol 6.

[43] INA §235(b)(1)(A)(i). For a detailed discussion of expedited removal, see CRS Report RL33109, *Immigration Policy on Expedited Removal of Aliens*, by Alison Siskin and Ruth Ellen Wasem.

[44] Under expedited removal, both administrative and judicial review are limited generally to cases in which the alien claims to be a U.S. citizen or to have been previously admitted as a legal permanent resident, a refugee, or an asylee.

[45] The INA provides immigration protections to aliens who have a well-founded fear of persecution, most notably in the form of asylum status. Aliens who are in expedited removal and claim asylum are given a "credible fear" hearing to determine if there is support for their asylum claim. Those who pass the credible fear hearing are placed into formal removal proceedings under INA §240. For a discussion of removal under §240 see Appendix A of CRS Report RL33109, *Immigration Policy on Expedited Removal of Aliens,* by Alison Siskin and Ruth Ellen Wasem. For more on credible fear, see CRS Report RL32621, *U.S. Immigration Policy on Asylum Seekers*, by Ruth Ellen Wasem.

[46] Due to the Homeland Security Act of 2002 (P.L. 107-296), expedited removal policy is being administered by the Secretary of Homeland Security.

[47] "Parole" is a term in immigration law which means that the alien has been granted temporary permission to enter and be present in the United States.

Parole does not constitute formal admission to the United States and parolees are required to leave when the parole expires, or if eligible, to be admitted in a lawful status.

[48] INA §241(a)(4)(A).

[49] Government Accountability Office, *Immigration Enforcement: Challenges to Implementing the INS Interior Enforcement Strategy*, (GAO-02-861T) June 19, 2002.

[50] If the alien is not a mandatory detainee and is not released on bond, the alien may request a bond redetermination hearing before an immigration judge to be given bond (if ICE denied release on bond) or to have the bond lowered. During the bond hearing, the alien must prove that he is not a flight risk or a danger to society.

[51] Examples of relief from deportation are voluntary departure, cancellation of removal, and asylum. While deportation may entail hardships to the alien and their family, these hardships alone do not exempt the alien from deportation, although they may have some influence on the granting of discretionary relief.

[52] An alien is inadmissible to the United States under §212(a)(6)(B) if he/she failed to attend his/her removal proceeding without "reasonable cause."

[53] INA §240(b)(7). Relief includes being able to adjust status, change nonimmigrant classification, or take advantage of the registry.

[54] INA §240(b).

[55] Aliens under voluntary departure must admit that their entry was illegal and waive their right to an immigration hearing. Aliens under voluntary departure may apply for legal entry in the future.

[56] DHS, *An Assessment of the Proposal to Merge Customs and Border Protection with Immigration and Customs Enforcement*, p. 27.

[57] Total time must be less than 120 days. 8 C.F.R. 240.25(c).

[58] DHS may revoke a grant of voluntary departure at any time. 8 C.F.R. 240.25(b).

[59] Press Office, Department of Homeland Security, U.S. Immigration and Customs Enforcement, *Ice Expands Pilot Project to Detain Deportable Aliens*, Mar. 26, 2004.

[60] See [http://www.ice.gov/graphics/about/organization/or_dro.htm] for more information on the Absconder Initiative. Testimony of Joseph R. Green, Assistant Commissioner for Investigations, Immigration and Naturalization Service, at House Judiciary Committee, Subcommittee on Immigration and Claims Hearing on INS Interior Enforcement (June 19, 2002).

[61] Failure to depart after the issuance of a final removal order is a felony under the INA.

[62] U.S. Department of Justice, Executive Office for Immigration Review, *FY2001-FY2005 Statistical Yearbook.*

[63] Stana, *Challenges to Implementing the Immigration Interior Enforcement Strategy*, p. 5.

[64] Of 35,318 criminal aliens released between 1994-1999, at least 11,605 went on to commit new crimes. See Governmental Accountability Office, *Criminal Aliens: INS' Efforts to Identify and Remove Imprisoned Aliens Continues to Need Improvement, (GAO/T-GGD-99-47), Feb. 25, 1999.*

[65] See CRS Report 96-601, *Immigration Enforcement Legislation: Overview of House and Senate Passed H.R. 2202*, by Larry M. Eig and Joyce C. Vialet. (Archived and available from the author.)

[66] The BIA backlog and its effect was the subject of a hearing in 2002. U.S. Congress, House Judiciary Committee, Subcommittee on Immigration and Claims, *The Operations of the Executive Office for Immigration Review (EOIR),* hearings, 107th Cong., 2nd sess., Feb. 6, 2002. (Hereafter cited as Hearing, *The Operations of the Executive Office for Immigration Review (EOIR).*)

[67] Special agents refers to personnel in the 1811 job series.

[68] Testimony of Joseph R. Green, Assistant Commissioner for Investigations, Immigration and Naturalization Service, at House Judiciary Committee, Subcommittee on Immigration and Claims Hearing on "INS Interior Enforcement," (June 19, 2002).

[69] Unpublished data from the Department of Homeland Security.

[70] For example, see Hearing, *The Operations of the Executive Office for Immigration Review (EOIR).*

[71] For example, see "Courts Criticize Judges' Handling of Asylum Cases," *New York Times*, Dec. 26, 2005; and Jason Ryan, "Attorney General Chastises Immigration Judges," *ABC News*, Jan. 11, 2006.

[72] For example see, Kirk Johnson, "Case Riles Colorado Town," *New York Times*, Dec. 13, 2004, p. A18.

[73] For example see, Luke Turf, "Return to Sender," *Denver Westwood*, Nov. 25, 2004.

[74] "Enemy combatants" at the Guantanamo U.S. military base in Cuba are not under the authority of DHS, nor are aliens incarcerated in federal, state, and local penitentiaries for criminal acts.

[75] Karen Musalo, et al., *The Expedited Removal Study Releases Its Third Report*, 77 Interpreted Releases 1189, 1191 (Aug. 21, 2000).

[76] Memorandum from Michael Pearson, INS Executive Associate Commissioner, Office of Field Operations, to Regional Directors, *Detention Guidelines Effective October 9, 1998*.

[77] High priority are aliens removable on security-related or criminal grounds who are not subject to required detention, and aliens who are a danger to the community or a flight risk. Medium priority detainees are inadmissible, non-criminal arriving aliens not in expedited removal and not subject to mandatory detention. Low priority detainees are other removable aliens not subject to required detention, and aliens who have committed fraud while applying for immigration benefits with DHS.

[78] There are some very limited exceptions to mandatory detention. An alien subject to mandatory detention may be released only if release is necessary to protect an alien who is a government witness in a major criminal investigation, or a close family member or associate of that alien, and the alien does not pose a danger to the public or a flight risk.

[79] Michael A. Pearson, *INS Detention Guidelines*, Oct. 7, 1998. Reprinted in *Bender's Immigration Bulletin*, vol. 3, no. 21, Nov. 1, 1998, p. 1111. (Hereafter cited as Pearson, *INS Detention Guidelines*.)

[80] P.L. 107-56, signed into law on Oct. 26, 2001.

[81] DHS, *An Assessment of the Proposal to Merge Customs and Border Protection with Immigration and Customs Enforcement*, p. 35.

[82] Department of Justice, Executive Office for Immigration Review, *FY2005 Statistical Yearbook*, Feb. 2006, p. H3.

[83] DHS, *An Assessment of the Proposal to Merge Customs and Border Protection with Immigration and Customs Enforcement*, p. 33.

[84] For a discussion of ICE's financial management issues, see CRS Report RL33049, *FY2006 Appropriations for Border and Transportation Security*, coordinated by Jennifer E. Lake and Blas Nuñez-Neto.

[85] U.S. Congress, Senate Committee on the Judiciary, Subcommittees on Immigration, Border Security, and Citizenship, and Terrorism, Technology and Homeland Security, *Strengthening Interior Enforcement: Deportation and Related Issues*, hearings, 109th Cong., 1st sess., Apr. 14, 2005.

[86] The decision does not usually apply to aliens who are under mandatory detention. A high priority detainee may be released to make space for a mandatory detainee. Nonetheless, DHS does have explicit procedures for choosing between two mandatory detainees if there is not enough bed space. Pearson, *INS Detention Guidelines*, p. 1116.

[87] Unpublished DHS data obtained from Betty Mills-Carilli, Bureau of Immigration and Customs Enforcement Office of Congressional Affairs, Department of Homeland Security, Apr. 8, 2004.

[88] DHS, *An Assessment of the Proposal to Merge Customs and Border Protection with Immigration and Customs Enforcement*, p. 32.

[89] Ibid., p. 38.

[90] Ibid., p. 4.

[91] The INA also establishes fines for transportation companies and employees of these companies (e.g., airlines, cruise lines, bus companies) who bring into the United States any alien who does not have a valid passport and, if required, an unexpired visa (§§271, 273).

[92] INA §§277, 278.

[93] In Dec. 2000, the United States and over 120 other countries signed the UN Convention against Transnational Organized Crime, and more than 75 of these countries signed the Protocol against the Smuggling of Migrants by Land, Sea and Air, which seeks to combat organized crime by harmonizing nations' criminal laws and promoting increased cooperation. Although the convention and the protocol have entered into force, the United States has not ratified the convention.

[94] Nonetheless, some ICE officers report that there has been a rise in smugglers holding the aliens hostage while extorting money from the alien's family. Personal communication with Patricia Schmidt, Assistant Special Agent in Charge, Phoenix Immigration and Customs Enforcement Office, Aug. 2, 2004.

[95] Controlled delivery is an investigative technique in which law enforcement knowingly allows a shipment to travel to its destination so that law enforcement can learn more about a criminal enterprise and the people involved.

[96] U.S. Government Accountability Office, *Combating Alien Smuggling, Opportunities Exist to Improve the Federal Response*, GAO-05-305, May 2005, p. 10. (Hereafter cited as GAO, *Combating Alien Smuggling, Opportunities Exist to Improve the Federal Response*.)

[97] Testimony of John P. Torres, Deputy Assistant Director, Smuggling and Public Safety, U.S. Immigration and Customs Enforcement, U.S. Department of Homeland Security, in U.S. Congress, House Committee on the Judiciary, Subcommittee on Immigration, Border Security, and Claims, *Pushing the Border Out on Alien Smuggling: New Tools and Intelligence Initiatives*, hearings, 108th Cong., 2nd sess., May 18, 2004. (Hereafter cited as Torres, *Pushing the Border Out on Alien Smuggling*.)

[98] Ibid.

[99] GAO, *Combating Alien Smuggling, Opportunities Exist to Improve the Federal Response.*

[100] Statement of Representative Linda T. Sanchez, in U.S. Congress, House Committee on the Judiciary, Subcommittee on Immigration, Border Security, and Claims, *Pushing the Border Out on Alien Smuggling: New Tools and Intelligence Initiatives*, hearings, 108th Cong., 2nd sess., May 18, 2004.

[101] Statement of Michael W. Cutler, Fellow, Center for Immigration Studies, in U.S. Congress, House Committee on the Judiciary, Subcommittee on Immigration, Border Security, and Claims, *Pushing the Border Out on Alien Smuggling: New Tools and Intelligence Initiatives*, hearings, 108th Cong., 2nd sess., May 18, 2004.

[102] Personal Communication with Kevin Burns, CFO University Medical Center, Aug. 3, 2004.

[103] Personal Communication with Sister Elizabeth, Humane Borders, Aug. 3, 2004.

[104] GAO, *Combating Alien Smuggling, Opportunities Exist to Improve the Federal Response*, p.4.

[105] 18 U.S.C. §1961.

[106] 18 U.S.C. §1956. GAO, *Combating Alien Smuggling, Opportunities Exist to Improve the Federal Response*, p.6.

[107] ICE and the Department of Justice have noted that there is a lack of statutory civil forfeiture authority for seizing real property (such as stash houses) which can hamper smuggling investigations.

[108] Governmental Accountability Office, *Alien Smuggling: Management and Operational Improvements Needed to Address Growing Problems* (GAO/GGD-00-103), May 1, 2000.

[109] GAO, *Immigration Enforcement: DHS Has Incorporated Immigration Enforcement Objectives and Is Addressing Future Planning Requirements (2004)*, p. 9.

[110] Personal communication with Immigration and Customs Enforcement Agents in Los Angeles, CA, Aug. 15, 2005.

[111] U.S. Immigration and Customs Enforcement website [http://www.bice.immigration.gov/graphics/enforce/invest/invest_hs.htm].

[112] U.S. Immigration and Customs Enforcement website [http://www.bice.immigration.gov/graphics/enforce/invest/invest_hs.htm].

[113] Testimony of Deputy Assistant Director, Smuggling and Public Safety, Bureau of Immigration and Customs Enforcement John P. Torres, in U.S.

Congress, House Judiciary Committee, Subcommittee on Immigration, Border Security, and Claims, *Alien Smuggling: New Tools and Intelligence Initiatives*, hearings, 108th Cong., 2nd sess., May 18, 2004. (Hereafter cited as Torres, *Alien Smuggling: New Tools.*)

[114] GAO, *Combating Alien Smuggling, Opportunities Exist to Improve the Federal Response*, p. 1.

[115] Testimony of Interim Associate Special Agent in Charge, Bureau of Immigration and Customs Enforcement Thomas Homan, in U.S. Congress, House Judiciary Committee, Subcommittee on Immigration, Border Security, and Claims, *The Deadly Consequences of Illegal Alien Smuggling* hearings, 108th Cong., 1st sess., June 24, 2003. (Hereafter cited as Homan, *Deadly Consequences*.)

[116] Torres, *Alien Smuggling: New Tools.*

[117] Testimony of Interim Assistant Director of Investigations, Bureau of Immigration and Customs Enforcement Charles H. Demore in U.S Congress, Senate Judiciary Committee, Subcommittee on Crime, Corrections, and Victims' Rights, *Alien Smuggling/Human Trafficking: Sending a Meaningful Message of Deterrence,* hearings, 108th Cong., 1st sess., July 25, 2003. (Hereafter cited as Demore, *Alien Smuggling/Human Trafficking.*)

[118] November 2004 MOU specified that the Border Patrol would actively prepare intelligence folders and forward them to ICE on a case- by-case basis as the need arises. GAO, *Combating Alien Smuggling, Opportunities Exist to Improve the Federal Response*, p. 14.

[119] Ibid., p. 11.

[120] Ibid., p. 3.

[121] Personal communication with Immigration and Customs Enforcement Agents and Customs and Border Patrol Agents, in Los Angeles and San Diego, CA, Aug. 15, 2005.

[122] GAO, *Alien Smuggling: Management and Operational Improvements Needed*, p. 5.

[123] The HSTC was established by the Intelligence Reform and Terrorist Prevention Act of 2004 (P.L. 108-408, §7202). See [http://www.state.gov/p/inl/c14079.htm].

[124] Stana, *Challenges to Implementing the Immigration Interior Enforcement Strategy*, pp. 5- 6.

[125] U.S. General Accounting Office (GAO), *Alien Smuggling: Management and Operational Improvements Needed to Address Growing Problem,*

GAO/GGD-00-103, May 2003, pp. 2-3. (Hereafter cited as GAO, *Alien Smuggling: Management and Operational Improvements Needed.*)

[126] GAO, *Immigration Enforcement: DHS Has Incorporated Immigration Enforcement Objectives and Is Addressing Future Planning Requirements*, p. 7.

[127] Marc Cooper, "Dead in Their Tracks," *LA Weekly*, Feb. 24, 2006, p. 32.

[128] Michael Riely, "Migrant-aid Case Puts Border Policy Under Microscope," *The Denver Post*, Jan. 2, 2006, p. A1.

[129] Lourdes Medrano, "Entrant Map Shows Border Roads, Water Tanks," *Arizona Daily Star*, Jan. 25, 2006.

[130] For legal analysis and legislative action pertaining to immigration document fraud, see CRS Report RL32657, *Immigration-Related Document Fraud: Overview of Civil, Criminal, and Immigration Consequences*, by Michael John Garcia.

[131] For a sample of discussions on the impact of breeder documents on immigration fraud, see U.S. House of Representatives, Committee on the Judiciary, Subcommittee on Immigration and Claims, *Hearing on Counterfeiting And Misuse Of the Social Security Card and State and Local Documents,* July 22, 1999; U.S. National Commission on Terrorist Attacks upon the United States, *The 9/11 Commission Report*, Executive Summary, July 2004; U.S. General Accounting Office, Report GAO-03-920, *Social Security Numbers: Improved SSN Verification and Exchange of States' Driver Records Would Enhance Identity Verifications*, September 2003; *New York Law Journal*, "Immigration Reform: Balancing Workers and Enforcement," by Stanley Mailman and Stephen Yale-Loehr, Aug. 2005; and, Center for Immigration Studies, *America's Identity Crisis: Document Fraud is Pervasive and Pernicious*, by Marti Dinerstein, Apr. 2002.

[132] U.S. House of Representatives, Committee on the Judiciary Subcommittee on Immigration and Claims, *Hearing on Visa Fraud and Immigration Benefits Application Fraud*, May 20, 1997.

[133] INA §212(c).

[134] INA §274(c).

[135] 18 U.S.C. §§1015, 1028.

[136] For example see U.S. Government Accountability Office (GAO), *Immigration Benefits: Additional Controls and a Sanctions Strategy Could Enhance DHS's Ability to Control Benefit Fraud*, GAO-06-259, Mar. 2006.

[137] P.L. 99-603. The changes made by Immigration Reform and Control Act of 1986 are discussed in more detail below.

[138] For a range of discussions, see U.S. House of Representatives, Committee on the Judiciary Subcommittee on Immigration and Claims, *Hearing on Visa Fraud and Immigration Benefits Application Fraud,* May 20, 1997; and Subcommittee on Immigration, Border Security, and Claims, *Hearing on John Allen Muhammad, Document Fraud, and the Western Hemisphere Passport Exception,* May 13, 2003.

[139] U.S. National Commission on Terrorist Attacks upon the United States, *The 9/11 Commission Report*, Executive Summary, July 2004; and *Monograph on 9/11 and Terrorist Travel*, Aug. 2004.

[140] U.S. House of Representatives, Committee on the Judiciary Subcommittee on Immigration and Claims, *Hearing on Visa Fraud and Immigration Benefits Application Fraud,* testimony of Paul Virtue, May 20, 1997.

[141] The five priorities (in rank order) were (1) identify and remove incarcerated criminal aliens from the United States and minimize recidivism; (2) deter, dismantle and diminish smuggling or trafficking of aliens; (3) respond to community reports and complaints about illegal immigration and build partnerships to solve local problems; (4) minimize immigration benefit fraud and other document abuse; and (5) block and remove employers' access to undocumented workers. U.S. Department of Justice Immigration and Naturalization Service, *Fact Sheet on Interior Enforcement*, February 2, 1999.

[142] U.S. Department of Justice Office of the Inspector General, Inspections Division, *Immigration and Naturalization Service Document Fraud Records Corrections*, Report Number I-96-09 September 1996; U.S. Senate Committee on the Judiciary Subcommittee on Technology, Terrorism, and Government Information, Statement of Glenn A. Fine, October 12, 2001; U.S. Government Accountability Office, GAO-02-830T, *Identity Fraud: Prevalence and Links to Alien Illegal Activities,* June 25, 2002; U.S. Government Accountability Office, GAO-03-660T, *Homeland Security: Challenges to Implementing the Immigration Interior Enforcement Strategy,* April 10, 2003; U.S. Government Accountability Office, GAO-05-66, *Immigration Enforcement: DHS Has Incorporated Immigration Enforcement Objectives and Is Addressing Future Planning Requirements*, October 8, 2004.

[143] U.S. Government Accountability Office, GAO-03-660T, *Homeland Security: Challenges to Implementing the Immigration Interior Enforcement Strategy*, April 10, 2003.

[144] For more discussion of inter-agency coordination issues, see CRS Report RL33319, *Toward More Effective Immigration Policies: Selected Organizational Issues*, by Ruth Ellen Wasem.

[145] U.S. Government Accountability Office, *Management Challenges Remain in Transforming Immigration Programs*, GAO-05-81, Oct. 2004.

[146] INA §§274A-274B.

[147] INA §274A, 8 U.S.C. §1324a. For further discussion of these legal provisions, see CRS Report RS22180, *Unauthorized Employment of Aliens: Basics of Employer Sanctions*, by Alison M. Smith. (Hereafter cited as CRS Report RS22180.)

[148] INA §274B, 8 U.S.C. §1324b. These provisions will not be discussed further here. See CRS Report RS22180. Additional information is also available at the OSC website [http://www.usdoj.gov/crt/osc/index.html].

[149] The Border Patrol also had a role in enforcing employer sanctions.

[150] U.S. Department of Justice, Immigration and Naturalization Service, "Second Report on the Implementation of IRCA," *INS Reporter*, summer 1989, pp. 2-3.

[151] U.S. Department of Justice, Immigration and Naturalization Service, "Employer Sanctions Program Policy," memorandum, April 5, 1991. The memorandum and accompanying implementation plan are reprinted in *Interpreter Releases*, vol. 68, no. 14 (April 15, 1991), pp. 445-455.

[152] Quoted in "INS Continues Enhanced Employer Sanctions Effort," *Interpreter Releases*, vol. 69, no. 8 (March 2, 1992), p. 253.

[153] U.S. President (Clinton), "Deterring Illegal Immigration," 60 *Federal Register* 7885-7889, Feb. 13, 1995.

[154] See CRS Report RS22180, *Unauthorized Employment of Aliens: Basics of Employer Sanctions*, by Alison M. Smith.

[155] U.S. Department of Justice, Immigration and Naturalization Service, "Immediate Action Directive for Worksite Enforcement Operations," memorandum, May 22, 1998. The memorandum and attachments are reprinted in *Interpreter Releases*, vol. 75, no. 27 (July 17, 1998), pp. 987-996.

[156] See William Branigin, "Criticism Prompts INS to Make New Rules for Work Site Raids; Some Fear Guidelines Will Limit Enforcement Capability," *Washington Post*, May 30, 1998, p. A2.

[157] According to the memorandum, worksite enforcement operations had to be approved by either a regional director or the Executive Associate Commissioner for Field Operations (or their designees), depending on the "sensitivity of the proposed operation."

[158] U.S. Department of Justice, Immigration and Naturalization Service, "Immediate Action Directive for Worksite Enforcement Operations," memorandum, May 22, 1998. The memorandum and attachments are reprinted in *Interpreter Releases*, vol. 75, no. 27 (July 17, 1998), pp. 987-996.

[159] U.S. Congress, House Committee on the Judiciary, Subcommittee on Immigration and Claims, *Immigration and Naturalization Service's Interior Enforcement Strategy*, 106th Cong., 1st sess., July 1, 1999 (Washington: GPO, 2000), p. 7. (Hereafter cited as 1999 House Hearing on INS's Interior Enforcement Strategy.)

[160] Ibid., p. 13.

[161] Ibid., p. 40.

[162] 2004 Senate Hearing on a Guest Worker Program, p. 66.

[163] See U.S. General Accountability Office, *Immigration Enforcement: Preliminary Observations on Employment Verification and Worksite Enforcement Efforts*, GAO-05-822T, June 21, 2005, p. 18. (Hereafter cited as 2005 GAO Testimony.)

[164] U.S. Department of Labor, Employment Standards Administration, and U.S. Department of Justice, Immigration and Naturalization Service, *Memorandum of Understanding Between the Immigration and Naturalization Service, Department of Justice, and the Employment Standards Administration, Department of Labor*, [1992]. Available in *Interpreter Releases*, vol. 69, no. 25 (July 6, 1992), pp. 829-833.

[165] See U.S. General Accountability Office, *Illegal Aliens: Significant Obstacles to Reducing Unauthorized Employment Exist*, GAO/GGD-99-33, April 1999, p. 19. (Hereafter cited as 1999 GAO report.)

[166] U.S. Department of Labor, Employment Standards Administration, and U.S. Department of Justice, Immigration and Naturalization Service, *Memorandum of Understanding Between the Immigration and Naturalization Service, Department of Justice, and the Employment Standards Administration, Department of Labor*, Nov. 23, 1998. Available in *Interpreter Releases*, vol. 75, no. 47 (Dec. 14, 1998), pp. 1711-1721.

[167] Employers have 30 days to request a hearing before an Administrative Law Judge in DOJ's Executive Office for Immigration Review (EOIR) to contest a NIF . If no hearing is requested, ICE issues a Final Order for civil money penalties. If a hearing is requested, the process may end in a Final Order, a settlement, or a dismissal.

[168] For information on current penalties, see CRS Report RS22180, *Unauthorized Employment of Aliens: Basics of Employer Sanctions*, by Alison M. Smith.

[169] These data were provided by ICE to the Senate Immigration Subcommittee as part of the agency's written response to questions following the February 2004 hearing. A CRS request for additional data is currently pending with ICE.

[170] INS noted criminal employer investigations require a greater expenditure of investigative hours than administrative [non-criminal] cases, and as a result, the number of administrative case completions, fines, and administrative arrests declined dramatically with the 1999 redirection. 2004 Senate Hearing on a Guest Worker Program, p. 65.

[171] *Fraudulent documents* refers here both to counterfeit documents and to genuine documents used fraudulently, such as by someone other than the individual to whom they were issued.

[172] Jeffrey S. Passel, *Unauthorized Migrants: Numbers and Characteristics*, Pew Hispanic Center, June 14, 2005, at [http://www.pewhispanic.org].

[173] For information about the guest worker issue, see CRS Report RL32044, *Policy Considerations Related to Guest Worker Programs*, by Andorra Bruno.

[174] For additional information on the Basic Pilot program, see U.S. Department of Homeland Security, U.S. Citizenship and Immigration Services, *Report to Congress on the Basic Pilot Program*, June 2004. This and other pilot program evaluation reports are available at [http://www.uscis.gov/graphics/aboutus/repsstudies/piloteval/PilotEval.htm]

[175] Reyes, *Holding the Line? The Effect of Recent Border Build-up on Unauthorized Immigration*, p. 80.

[176] Testimony of Richard M. Stana, Director of Justice Issues, GAO, at House Judiciary Committee, Subcommittee on Immigration and Claims Hearing on "INS Interior Enforcement," June 19, 2002.

[177] Steven Greenhouse, "U.S. Officials Defend Ploys to Catch Immigrants," *New York Times*, Feb. 11, 2006, p. A8.

[178] Testimony of Acting Administrator, Wage and Hour Division, Department of Labor, John R. Fraser, in U.S. Congress, House Committee on the Judiciary, Subcommittee on Immigration and Claims, *Oversight hearing on the Immigration and Naturalization Service's Interior Enforcement Strategy,* hearings, 106th Cong., 1st sess., July 1, 1999.

[179] Reyes, *Holding the Line? The Effect of Recent Border Build-up on Unauthorized Immigration*, p. 83.

[180] Testimony of Executive Director of the Center of Immigration Studies, Mark Krikorian, in U.S. Congress, House Judiciary Committee, Subcommittee on Immigration, Border Security, and Claims, *Department of Homeland Security Transition: Bureau of Immigration and Customs Enforcement*, hearings, 108th Cong., 1st sess., Apr. 10, 2003. (Hereafter cited as Krikorian, *Department of Homeland Security Transition: Bureau of Immigration and Customs Enforcement.*)

[181] Testimony of Barbara D. Bocbjerg, Director Education, Workforce, and Income Security Issues, Government Accountability Office, in U.S. Congress, Ways and Means Committee, Subcommittees on Social Security and on Oversight, *Second in a Series of Hearings on Social Security Number High Risk Issues*, hearings, 109th Cong., 2nd sess., Feb. 16, 2006.

[182] "Social Security No-Match Letter," *Interpreter Releases*, vol. 80, Apr. 7, 2003, pp. 508-509.

[183] Ibid., p. 508.

[184] Mary Beth Sheridan, "Social Security Scales Back Worker Inquiries," *Washington Post*, June 18, 2003, p. A6. No-match letters for tax year 2001 were sent in calendar year 2002.

[185] Unpublished data from SSA.

[186] While CBP inspectors conduct other types of inspections (i.e., custom and animal and plant health inspections), only immigration inspections are discussed in this report. For additional information on CBP inspections, see CRS Report RL32399, *Border Security: Inspections Practices, Policies, and Issues*, by Ruth Ellen Wasem, Coordinator, Jennifer Lake, Lisa M. Seghetti, James Monke, and Stephen Vina.

[187] §235 of the INA.

[188] Section 123 of the Illegal Immigration Reform and Immigrant Responsibility Act of 1996 (IIRIRA; P.L. 104-208) required the Attorney General to establish preinspection stations in at least five foreign airports that are identified as being one of ten foreign airports that serve as the last point of departure for the greatest number of inadmissible aliens.

[189] §287(b)(c) of the INA.

[190] 11 Lookout databases contain information on aliens who are inadmissible for entry into the United States.

[191] CRS analysis of the former Immigration and Naturalization Service (INS) PAS data. During the years examined, the former INS tracked the hours immigration inspectors spent on several activities, including enforcing immigration law. CRS also included hours spent on processing expedited removal cases and escorting aliens (detention duty) as enforcement hours.

[192] At some ports of entry (i.e., San Ysidro), senior level immigration inspectors perform investigative activities.

[193] IBIS is an interagency inspections system that is used by immigration inspectors at ports of entry to verify and obtain information on aliens presenting themselves for entry into the United States. IBIS is a broad system that interfaces with other data systems and databases, and thus, is able to obtain such information as whether an alien is admissible, an alien's criminal information, and whether an alien is wanted by law enforcement.

[194] IDENT is an immigration system used by inspectors during primary inspections and ICE agents when they come into contact with aliens. IDENT is composed of two databases: (1) a "lookout" database that contains fingerprints and photographs of aliens who have been previously deported or have a criminal history; and (2) a "recidivist" database that contains fingerprints and photographs of illegal aliens who have been apprehended by the border patrol.

[195] The FBI's NCIC III is a computerized index of criminal information on individuals who have come into contact with the law enforcement community. Fingerprint information is submitted to the FBI by participating federal, state and local law enforcement agencies. NCIC III also contains names of wanted persons as well as the names of violent gangs and terrorists. NCIC interfaces with IBIS.

[196] CBP's Passenger Analysis Unit is an automated targeting system, located at ports of entry, that is based on strategic intelligence about threats. This system identifies individuals who may need to be more closely scrutinized.

[197] P.L. 109-13.

[198] For evaluations, see U.S. General Accounting Office, *Information Technology: Terrorist Watch Lists Should Be Consolidated to Promote Better Integration and Sharing*, GAO-03-322, Apr. 15, 2003; and U.S. General Accounting Office, *Border Security: Challenges in Implementing Border Technology*, GAO-03-546T, Mar. 12, 2003.

[199] For a full discussion of US-VISIT, see CRS Report RL32234, *U.S. Visitor and Immigrant Status Indicator Technology Program (US-VISIT)*, by Lisa M. Seghetti and Stephen R. Vina.

[200] Other categories of foreign nationals that are currently exempt from the requirements of the program include (1) certain visa categories, such as those for diplomats, ambassadors, and foreign government employees and their families who are in transit; (2) other classes of visitors the Secretaries of State and Homeland Security jointly determine should be exempt; and (3) children under the age of 14 and senior over the age of 79.

[201] U.S. Congress, House Committee on the Judiciary, Subcommittee on Immigration, Border Security, and Claims, oversight hearing on *Funding for Immigration in the President's 2005 Budget*, testimony of Seth Stodder, Feb. 25, 2004.

[202] See §212 of INA *and* 21 C.F.R.

[203] See P.L. 108-458.

[204] See 21 C.F.R.

[205] For a more detailed analysis of the U.S. Border Patrol, please refer to CRS Report RL32562, *Border Security: The Role of the U.S. Border Patrol*, by Blas Nunez-Neto.

[206] INA §275(a). The first offense under this statute is a fine or imprisonment for not more than six months, or both. The penalty for any subsequent offenses under the statute is fine or imprisonment for not more than two years, or both.

[207] The USBP does not patrol the border between Alaska and Canada; for the purposes of this report the Northern border is the border between the contiguous United States and Canada.

[208] U.S. General Accounting Office, *Border Security: Agencies Need to Better Coordinate Their Strategies and Operations on Federal Lands*, GAO-04-590, June 2004, pp.10-11. Testimony of George Regan, Acting Associate Commissioner, Enforcement, Immigration and Naturalization Service, in U.S. Congress, House Committee on the Judiciary, Subcommittee on Immigration and Claims, *Combating Illegal Immigration: Progress Report*, 105th Cong., 1st sess., Apr. 23, 1997.

[209] Department of Homeland Security, Bureau of Customs and Border Protection, "National Border Patrol Strategy," Mar. 1, 2005.

[210] Ibid.

[211] Ibid., p. 3.

[212] Apprehensions have long been used as a performance measure by the USBP. However, it is impossible to gauge solely from apprehensions data whether increases or decreases in apprehensions are due to unauthorized migration patterns or border enforcement policies and resources. An increase in apprehensions could be due to an increase in the number of unauthorized migrants attempting to enter the country. The same increase could also be due to increased patrolling of the border, as the additional agents make more arrests. Or it could be due to both an increase in the number of people attempting to illegally enter the country and increased patrolling. Lastly, it could be due to neither, and merely be a statistical anomaly.

[213] For additional information, see CRS Report RL32270, *Enforcing Immigration Law: The Role of State and Local Law Enforcement*, by Lisa M. Seghetti, Stephen R. Vina and Karma Ester.

[214] According to DHS Congressional Affairs Office, as of Feb. 25, 2005, there are 5,500 ICE agents.

[215] Currently, DHS has entered into four MOUs, with the states of Florida and Alabama, the Los Angeles, California Sheriff Department, and the state of Arizona.

[216] For example see the Clear Law Enforcement for Criminal Alien Removal (CLEAR) Act of 2005 (H.R. 3137); the Homeland Security Enhancement Act of 2005 (S. 1362); the Save America Comprehensive Immigration Act of 2005 (H.R. 2092); Comprehensive Enforcement and Immigration Reform Act of 2005 (H.R. 1438); Rewarding Employers that Abide by the Law and Guaranteeing Uniform Enforcement to Stop Terrorism Act of 2005 (H.R. 3333); Scott Gardner Act (H.R. 3776); and the Enforcement First Immigration Reform Act of 2005 (H.R. 3938).

[217] Testimony of U.S. Immigration and Customs Enforcement, in U.S. Congress, Senate Committee on the Judiciary, Subcommittee on Immigration, Border Security and Citizenship, *State and Local Authority to Enforce Immigration Law: Evaluating a United Approach to Stop Terrorists*, hearings, 108th Cong., 2nd sess., Apr. 22, 2004.

[218] Testimony of Human Rights Watch, in U.S. Congress, Senate Committee on the Judiciary Subcommittee on Immigration, Border Security and Citizenship, *State and Local Authority to Enforce Immigration Law: Evaluating a United Approach to Stop Terrorists*, 108th Cong., 2nd sess., Apr. 22, 2004.

[219] Testimony of Marisa Demeo, Regional Counsel, Mexican American Legal Defense Fund, House Judiciary Committee, Subcommittee on Immigration and Claims, *INS Interior Enforcement*, hearings, 107th Cong., 2nd sess., June 19, 2002.

[220] Ibid.

[221] For an example of this argument, see interview with Gene Voegtlin, legislative counsel for the International Association of Chiefs of Police, in Miriam Jorden, "Cities and States Take on Difficult Duty of Handling Undocumented Workers," *The Wall Street Journal*, Feb. 2, 2006, p. B1.

[222] A workyear is equal to 2,080 hours of work and represents the work performed by one full-time investigator in a year.

[223] DHS, *An Assessment of the Proposal to Merge Customs and Border Protection with Immigration and Customs Enforcement*, p. 1.

[224] As explained by former DHS Under Secretary for Border and Transportation Security Asa Hutchinson in written response to questions from the Senate Judiciary Committee's Subcommittee on Immigration, Border Security and Citizenship, resources from worksite enforcement and other enforcement activities were diverted in the 1990s to locate and remove criminal aliens.

[225] U.S. Congress, Senate Committee on the Judiciary, Subcommittee on Immigration, Border Security and Citizenship, *Evaluating a Temporary Guest Worker Program*, 108th Cong., 2nd sess., Feb. 12, 2004 (Washington: GPO, 2004), p. 66. (Hereafter cited as 2004 Senate Hearing on a Guest Worker Program).

[226] U.S. Department of Justice, Immigration and Naturalization Service, "Immediate Action Directive for Worksite Enforcement Operations," memorandum, May 22, 1998. The memorandum and attachments are reprinted in *Interpreter Releases*, vol. 75, no. 27 (July 17, 1998), pp. 987-996.

[227] See William Branigin, "Criticism Prompts INS to Make New Rules for Work Site Raids; Some Fear Guidelines Will Limit Enforcement Capability," *Washington Post*, May 30, 1998, p. A2.

[228] GAO, *Combating Alien Smuggling, Opportunities Exist to Improve the Federal Response*, p. 23.

[229] Robert Warren, of the former INS, estimated that the unauthorized population was 3.4 million in 1992, and Jeffery Passel, currently of the Pew Hispanic Center, estimated that the unauthorized population was 9.3 million in 2002 and 10.3 million in 2004. For a full discussion of these estimates see CRS Report RS21938, *Unauthorized Aliens in the United States: Estimates Since 1986*, by Ruth Ellen Wasem.

[230] CRS analysis of the former Immigration and Naturalization Service (INS) PAS data. During the years examined, the former INS tracked the hours immigration inspectors spent on several activities, including enforcing immigration law. CRS also included hours spent on processing expedited removal cases and escorting aliens (detention duty) as enforcement hours.

[231] See CRS Report RL32562, *Border Security: The Role of the U.S. Border Patrol*, by Blas Nunez-Neto.

[232] For example see U.S. Congress, Senate Committee on Homeland Security and Governmental Affairs, *The Department of Homeland Security: The Road Ahead*, 109th Cong., 1st sess., Jan. 26, 2005; U.S. Congress, House Homeland Security Committee, Subcommittee on Management, Integration, and Oversight, *CBP and ICE: Does the Current Organizational Structure*

Best Serve U.S. Homeland Security Interests? 109th Cong., 1st sess., Mar. 9, 2005; and U.S. Congress, House Homeland Security Committee, Subcommittee on Management, Integration, and Oversight, *CBP and ICE: Does the Current Organizational Structure Best Serve U.S. Homeland Security Interests? Part 2*, 109th Cong., 1st sess., Nov. 15, 2005.

[233] GAO, *Immigration Enforcement: DHS Has Incorporated Immigration Enforcement Objectives and Is Addressing Future Planning Requirements*, p. 7.

[234] For example, see U.S. Government Accountability Office (GAO), *Criminal Aliens: INS' Efforts to Identify and Remove Imprisoned Aliens Continue to Need Improvement*, GAO/T-GGD-99-47, Feb. 25, 1999; U.S. Government Accountability Office, *Illegal Aliens: Significant Obstacles to Reducing Unauthorized Alien Employment Exist*, GAO/GGD-99-33, Apr. 2, 1999; U.S. Government Accountability Office, *Alien Smuggling: Management and Operational Improvements Needed to Address Growing Problem*, GAO/GGD-00-103, May 1, 2000; U.S. Government Accountability Office, *Immigration Benefit Fraud: Focused Approach Is Needed to Address Problems*, GAO-02-66, Jan. 31, 2002.

[235] Testimony of Richard M. Stana, Director of Justice Issues, GAO, U.S. Congress, House Judiciary Committee, Subcommittee on Immigration and Claims, *INS Interior Enforcement*, hearings, 107th Cong., 2nd sess., June 19, 2002.

[236] Stana, *Addressing Management Challenges that Face Immigration Enforcement Agencies*, p. 2.

[237] Government Accountability Office, *Homeland Security: Challenges to Implementing Interior Enforcement Strategy*, Apr. 10, 2003 (GAO-03-660T).

[238] Testimony of Director Homeland Security and Justice Issues, Government Accountability Office, Richard M. Stana, in U.S. Congress, House Judiciary Committee, Subcommittee on Immigration, Border Security, and Claims, *Challenges to Implementing the Immigration Interior Enforcement Strategy*, hearings, 108th Cong., 1st sess., Apr. 10, 2003, GAO-03-660T, p. 1. (Hereafter cited as Stana, *Challenges to Implementing the Immigration Interior Enforcement Strategy*.)

[239] Ibid., p. 6.

[240] Government Accountability Office, *Homeland Security: Challenges to Implementing Interior Enforcement Strategy*, Apr. 10, 2003 (GAO-03-660T).

[241] Testimony of Director Homeland Security and Justice Issues, Government Accountability Office, Richard M. Stana, in U.S. Congress, House Judiciary Committee, Subcommittee on Immigration. Border Security, and Claims, *Addressing Management Challenges that Face Immigration Enforcement Agencies,* 109th Cong., 1st sess., May 5, 2005, (GAO-05-664T), p. 13. (Hereafter cited as Stana, *Addressing Management Challenges that Face Immigration Enforcement Agencies.*)

[242] For example see Government Accountability Office, *Immigration and Naturalization Service: Overview of Recurring Management Challenges,* Oct. 17, 2001 (GAO-02-168T); Government Accountability Office, *Information Technology: Terrorist Watchlists Should be Consolidated to Promote Better Integration and Information Sharing,* Apr. 2003 (GAO-03-322); and Department of Justice, Office of the Inspector General, Status of *IDENT/IAFIS Integration*, June 2003 (I-2003-005).

[243] P.L. 107-173.

[244] U.S. Congress, Senate Committee on the Judiciary Subcommittee on Technology, Terrorism and Government Information, *Border Technology: Keeping Terrorists Out of the United States — 2003*, hearing, Mar. 12, 2003.

[245] As discussed above, most aliens apprehended by border patrol take voluntary departure rather than undergo the formal removal process. DHS *An Assessment of the Proposal to Merge Customs and Border Protection with Immigration and Customs Enforcement*, p. 3.

[246] Stana, *Addressing Management Challenges that Face Immigration Enforcement Agencies*, p. 5.

[247] U.S. Government Accountability Office, *Immigration Enforcement: DHS Has Incorporated Immigration Enforcement Objectives and Is Addressing Future Planning Requirements*, GAO-05-66, Oct. 2004, p. 5. (Hereafter cited as GAO, *Immigration Enforcement: DHS Has Incorporated Immigration Enforcement Objectives and Is Addressing Future Planning Requirements.*)

[248] Stana, *Challenges to Implementing the Immigration Interior Enforcement Strategy*, p. 10.

[249] Meeting with ICE presentation.

[250] In Oct. 2005, the Directorate of Border and Transportation Security was abolished, and ICE and CBP were placed directly under the Secretary of Homeland Security. For more information on the organization and restructuring of immigration functions within DHS, see CRS Report

RL33319, *Toward More Effective Immigration Policies: Selected Organizational Issues*, by Ruth Ellen Wasem.

[251] Department of Homeland Security, Office of Inspector General, *An Assessment of the Proposal to Merge Customs and Border Protection with Immigration and Customs Enforcement*, Nov. 2005, p. 2. (Hereafter cited as DHS, *An Assessment of the Proposal to Merge Customs and Border Protection with Immigration and Customs Enforcement*.)

[252] Ibid., p. 3.

[253] Ibid., pp. 6, 10.

[254] Ibid., pp. 19-20.

[255] Testimony of Stewart Baker, Assistant Secretary of Policy, Department of Homeland Security, in U.S. Congress, House Homeland Security Committee, Subcommittee on Management, Integration, and Oversight, *CBP and ICE: Does the Current Organizational Structure Best Serve U.S. Homeland Security Interests? Part 2*, 109th Cong., 1st sess., Nov. 15, 2005.

[256] DHS, *An Assessment of the Proposal to Merge Customs and Border Protection with Immigration and Customs Enforcement*, p. 5.

[257] Ibid., p. 45.

[258] Stana, *Challenges to Implementing the Immigration Interior Enforcement Strategy*, p. 11.

[259] DHS, *An Assessment of the Proposal to Merge Customs and Border Protection with Immigration and Customs Enforcement*, p.6.

[260] Ibid., pp. 6, 13.

[261] For an example of this agreement see, Douglas S. Massey, *Backfire at the Border: Why Enforcement Without Legalization Cannot Stop Illegal Immigration*, Cato Institute, June 13, 2005.

[262] Mark Krikorian, *Giving Enforcement a Chance: Before We Give Up on Immigration Enforcement, Why Don't We Try It?* (Washington, Center for Immigration Studies, Feb. 2006).

[263] INA §202(a)(2) establishes per-country ceiling at 7% of the worldwide level.

[264] See CRS Report RL32235, *U.S. Immigration Policy on Permanent Admissions*, by Ruth Ellen Wasem.

[265] For example see, T. Alexander Alienikoff, "Legal Immigration Reform: Toward Rationality and Equity," in Richard D. Lamm and Alan Simpson, eds., *Blue Prints for an Ideal Legal Immigration Policy,* Center for Immigration Studies, Center Paper #17, Mar. 2001.

[266] *Federal Register*, Mar. 7, 2003, vol. 68, no. 45, pp. 10954-10957.

[267] For a full discussion see CRS Report RL32044, *Immigration: Policy Considerations Related to Guest Worker Programs*, by Andorra Bruno.

[268] Mark Krikorian, *Giving Enforcement a Chance: Before We Give Up on Immigration Enforcement, Why Don't We Try It?* (Washington, Center for Immigration Studies, Feb. 2006).

[269] Some local law enforcement agencies have used local laws, such as laws against trespassing and the housing codes, to arrest unauthorized aliens. For example see, Dan McLean, "Police Outline Prosecution of 'Trespassing' Alien," *Union Leader*, June 29, 2005, p. A1; and Patrik Jonsson, "To Curb Illegal Immigration, South Cracks Down on Housing Codes," *Christian Science Monitor*, Jan. 16, 2006.

In: Immigration Enforcement and Policies
Editor: B. T. Isenburg, pp. 95-140
ISBN: 1-60021-303-0

Chapter 2

IMMIGRATION: POLICY CONSIDERATIONS RELATED TO GUEST WORKER PROGRAMS*

Andorra Bruno

ABSTRACT

At present, the United States has two main programs for temporarily importing low-skilled workers, sometimes referred to as guest workers. Agricultural guest workers enter through the H-2A visa program, and other guest workers enter through the H-2B visa program. Employers interested in importing workers under either program must first apply to the U.S. Department of Labor for a certification that U.S. workers capable of performing the work are not available and that the employment of alien workers will not adversely affect the wages and working conditions of similarly employed U.S. workers. Other requirements of the programs differ.

The 109th Congress has enacted language as part the FY2005 Emergency Supplemental Appropriations Act (P.L. 109-13) to revise the H-2B program. Other bills before the 109th Congress propose to make changes to the H-2A program (S. 359/H.R. 884, H.R. 3857, S. 2087, Specter substitute to S. 2454), the H-2B program (S. 278, H.R. 1587, S. 1438, S. 1918), and the "H" visa category generally (H.R. 3333), and to establish new temporary worker visas (S. 1033/H.R. 2330, S. 1438, S. 1918, H.R. 4065, Specter substitute to S. 2454). S. 359/H.R. 884, S. 1033/H.R. 2330, S. 1918, and the Specter substitute to S. 2454 also would establish mechanisms for certain foreign workers to become U.S. legal permanent residents (LPRs). Various guest

* Excerpted from CRS Report RL32044, dated April 6, 2006.

worker measures were introduced in the 108th Congress, but they saw no action beyond committee referrals. President George W. Bush proposed a new, expanded guest worker program in January 2004 when he announced his principles for immigration reform.

The current discussion of guest worker programs takes place against a backdrop of historically high levels of unauthorized migration to the United States. Supporters of a large-scale temporary worker program argue that such a program would help reduce unauthorized immigration by providing a legal alternative for prospective foreign workers. Critics reject this reasoning and instead maintain that a new guest worker program would likely exacerbate the problem of illegal migration.

The consideration of any proposed guest worker program raises various issues, including the following: how new program requirements would compare with those of the H-2A and H-2B programs; program eligibility; inclusion of a program mechanism for participants to obtain LPR status; how family members of eligible individuals would be treated; what labor market test, if any, the program would employ; whether the program would be numerically limited; how the rules and requirements of the program would be enforced; and what security-related provisions, if any, would be included.

INTRODUCTION

In 2001, the United States and Mexico began Cabinet-level talks on migration. Although the details of these discussions were not made public, two issues —legalization and a temporary worker program — dominated media coverage. The talks lost momentum after the terrorist attacks of September 11, 2001, as the Bush Administration focused its attention on security-related matters. A temporary worker program (not limited to Mexico), however, remains of interest to some Members of Congress and Administration officials. Various bills to reform existing programs for foreign temporary workers and to create new temporary worker programs have been introduced in recent Congresses. Several such bills are before the 109th Congress. In January 2004, the Bush Administration outlined a proposal for a new temporary worker program. The new programs under discussion presumably would cover largely low-skilled workers.

BACKGROUND

The term *guest worker* has typically been applied to foreign temporary low-skilled laborers, often in agriculture or other seasonal employment. In the past, guest worker programs have been established in the United States to address worker shortages during times of war. During World War I, for example, tens of thousands of Mexican workers performed mainly agricultural labor as part of a temporary worker program. The Bracero program, which began during World War II and lasted until 1964, brought several million Mexican agricultural workers into the United States. At its peak in the late 1950s, the Bracero program employed more than 400,000 Mexican workers annually.[1]

The Immigration and Nationality Act (INA) of 1952, as originally enacted,[2] authorized a temporary foreign worker program known as the H-2 program. It covered both agricultural and nonagricultural workers who were coming temporarily to the United States to perform temporary services (other than services of an exceptional nature requiring distinguished merit and ability) or labor. Aliens who are admitted to the United States for a temporary period of time and a specific purpose are known as nonimmigrants. The 1986 Immigration Reform and Control Act (IRCA)[3] amended the INA to subdivide the H-2 program into the current H-2A and H-2B programs and to detail the admissions process for H-2A workers. The H-2A and H-2B visas are subcategories of the larger "H" nonimmigrant visa category for temporary workers.[4]

CURRENT PROGRAMS

The United States currently has two main programs for importing temporary low-skilled workers. Agricultural workers enter through the H-2A program and other temporary workers enter through the H-2B program.[5] The programs take their names from the sections of the INA that established them — Section 101(a)(15)(H)(ii)(a) and Section 101(a)(15)(H)(ii)(b), respectively. Both programs are administered by the Employment and Training Administration (ETA) of the U.S. Department of Labor (DOL) and U.S. Citizenship and Immigration Services (USCIS) of the U.S. Department of Homeland Security (DHS).[6]

H-2A Program

The H-2A program allows for the temporary admission of foreign workers to the United States to perform agricultural work of a seasonal or temporary nature, provided that U.S. workers are not available. An approved H-2A visa petition is generally valid for an initial period of up to one year.[7] An alien's total period of stay as an H-2A worker may not exceed three consecutive years.

Employers who want to import H-2A workers must first apply to DOL for a certification that (1) there are not sufficient U.S. workers who are qualified and available to perform the work; and (2) the employment of foreign workers will not adversely affect the wages and working conditions of U.S. workers who are similarly employed. As part of this labor certification process, employers must attempt to recruit U.S. workers and must cooperate with DOL-funded state employment service agencies (also known as state workforce agencies) in local, intrastate, and interstate recruitment efforts. Employers must pay their H-2A workers and similarly employed U.S. workers the highest of the federal or applicable state minimum wage, the prevailing wage rate,[8] or the adverse effect wage rate (AEWR).[9] They also must provide workers with housing, transportation, and other benefits, including workers' compensation insurance.[10] No health insurance coverage is required.[11]

Both growers and labor advocates criticize the H-2A program in its current form. Growers complain that the H-2A program is overly cumbersome and does not meet their labor needs. Labor advocates argue that the program provides too few protections for U.S. workers.

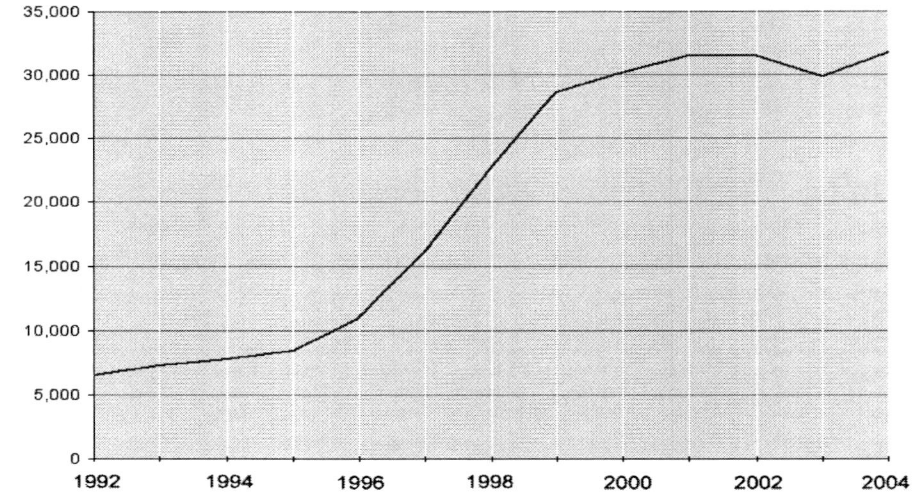

Figure 1. H-2A Visas Issued, FY1992-FY2004.

H-2A Visas Issued

The H-2A program, which is not subject to numerical limits, has grown almost fivefold over the last decade. As illustrated in Figure 1, the number of H-2A visas, which are issued abroad by the Department of State (DOS), increased from 6,445 in FY1992 to 30,201 in FY2000, and has remained at about 30,000 annually since then. In FY2004, DOS issued 31,774 H-2A visas. According to preliminary data, 31,892 H-2A visas were issued in FY2005. The H-2A program, however, remains quite small relative to total U.S. agricultural employment, which stood at 3.2 million in 2002, according to DOL's Bureau of Labor Statistics.

H-2B Program

The H-2B program provides for the temporary admission of foreign workers to the United States to perform temporary non-agricultural work, if unemployed U.S. workers cannot be found. Foreign medical graduates coming to perform medical services are explicitly excluded from the program. An approved H-2B visa petition is valid for an initial period of up to one year.[12] An alien's total period of stay as an H-2B worker may not exceed three consecutive years.[13]

Like prospective H-2A employers, prospective H-2B employers must first apply to DOL for a certification that U.S. workers capable of performing the work are not available and that the employment of alien workers will not adversely affect the wages and working conditions of similarly employed U.S. workers. H-2B employers must pay their workers at least the prevailing wage rate. Unlike H-2A employers, they are not subject to the AEWR and do not have to provide housing, transportation,[14] and other benefits required under the H-2A program.

USCIS has proposed regulations aimed at streamlining the H-2B petitioning process, which would significantly alter procedures.[15] Among other changes, the proposed rule, published in the *Federal Register* on January 27, 2005, would eliminate the requirement that prospective H-2B employers file for a labor certification from DOL in most cases. Instead, employers seeking H-2B workers in areas other than logging, the entertainment industry, and professional athletics would include certain labor attestations as part of the H-2B petition they file with USCIS.

According to the proposed rule, this H-2B attestation process would be similar to the process currently used for H-1B professional specialty workers.[16]

A key limitation of the H-2B visa concerns the requirement that the work be temporary. Under the applicable immigration regulations, work is considered to be temporary if the employer's need for the duties to be performed by the worker is a one-time occurrence, seasonal need, peakload need, or intermittent need.[17] According to DOL data on H-2B labor certifications, the top five H-2B occupations in FY2004, in terms of the number of workers certified, were: (1)

landscape laborer, (2) forestry worker, (3) maids and housekeeping cleaners, (4) construction worker, and (5) stable attendant.

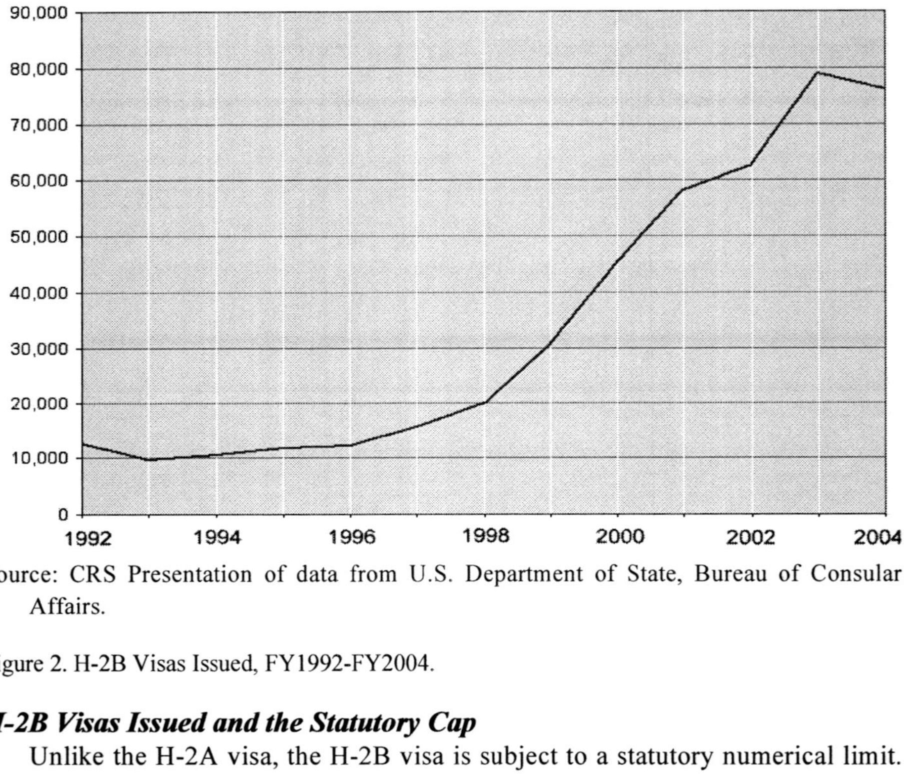

Source: CRS Presentation of data from U.S. Department of State, Bureau of Consular Affairs.

Figure 2. H-2B Visas Issued, FY1992-FY2004.

H-2B Visas Issued and the Statutory Cap

Unlike the H-2A visa, the H-2B visa is subject to a statutory numerical limit. Under the INA, the total number of aliens who may be issued H-2B visas or otherwise provided H-2B status during a fiscal year may not exceed 66,000.[18] This cap does not apply to all H-2B petitions. Petitions for current H-2B workers to extend their stay, change their terms of employment, or change or add employers do not count towards the cap. As shown in Figure 2, the number of H-2B visas issued by DOS dipped from 12,552 in FY1992 to 9,691 in FY1993 and then began to increase steadily.

In FY2003, DOS issued 78,955 H-2B visas, and in FY2004, it issued 76,169 H-2B visas. While for various reasons not all visas issued during a fiscal year necessarily count against that year's cap or, in some cases, any year's cap, USCIS acknowledged that the H-2B cap was exceeded in FY2003. With respect to the FY2004 cap, USCIS announced on March 10, 2004, that it had received a sufficient number of H-2B petitions to meet that cap. On January 4, 2005, it announced that the FY2005 cap had been reached. It indicated that it would process all petitions received by January 3, 2005, but would not accept any new H-2B petitions subject to the FY2005 cap after that date.[19]

Following the enactment of new H-2B provisions as part of the FY2005 Emergency Supplemental Appropriations Act for Defense, the Global War on Terror, and Tsunami Relief (P.L. 109-13) (see discussion below of S. 352/H.R. 793 in the 109th Congress), USCIS announced that on May 25, 2005, it would start accepting additional petitions for H-2B workers for FY2005.[20] Under P.L. 109-13, for FY2005 and FY2006, returning H-2B workers counted against the annual 66,000 cap during any one of the three prior fiscal years cannot be counted again. USCIS determined that approximately 35,000 previously approved H-2B workers for FY2005 qualified as returning workers who, under P.L. 109-13, were exempt from that year's cap, opening up 35,000 slots for other H-2B workers. Employers were able to file FY2005 petitions for new H-2B workers to fill those slots, as well as for cap-exempt returning H-2B workers. According to preliminary data, 87,492 H-2B visas were issued in FY2005.

UNAUTHORIZED IMMIGRATION

The current discussion of guest worker programs has been prompted, in part, by the continued high levels of illegal, or unauthorized, immigration to the United States and related deaths along the U.S.-Mexican border. Analyses based on data from the Current Population Survey (CPS) and other sources estimate that the unauthorized resident alien population totaled 9.3 million in March 2002, 10.3 million in March 2004, and 11.1 million in March 2005; since 2000, this population has grown at an average annual rate of more than 500,000 per year.[21] DHS has not published a recent estimate of the unauthorized alien population. The former INS estimated that in January 2000 there were about 7.0 million unauthorized aliens residing in the United States based on data from the 2000 census of the U.S. population and other sources.[22]

Mexico remains the largest source country for unauthorized immigration. According to the recent estimates, the unauthorized Mexican population in the United States was about 5.3 million in 2002, 5.9 million in 2004, and 6.2 million in 2005, comprising 56% or 57% of the total unauthorized population in each of the years. With respect to migrant deaths, data from the DHS indicate that more than 300 migrants died at the U.S.-Mexican border each year from FY2000 through FY2004.[23]

Unauthorized Workers

Unauthorized workers are a subpopulation of the total unauthorized alien population. In the March 2006 report cited above, the Pew Hispanic Center estimated that there were about 7.2 million unauthorized workers in the U.S. civilian labor force in March 2005.[24] These workers represented about 4.9% of the labor force. In some occupations and industries, however, their share of the labor force was considerably higher. According to the report:

> Unauthorized workers are employed in a variety of occupations throughout the labor force, although the distribution of the unauthorized workforce across occupations differs from that of native-born workers.
> Unauthorized workers are notably underrepresented in white-collar occupations.... On the other hand, unauthorized migrants are much more likely to be in major occupation groups that require little education or do not have licensing requirements.[25]

Unauthorized aliens are also overrepresented in certain industries relative to their share of the overall labor force. Table 1 presents data from the Pew Hispanic Center report on industries with high concentrations of unauthorized workers. Unauthorized aliens accounted for between 10% and 21% of workers in the industries shown.

Table 1. Estimates of Unauthorized Employment in Selected Industries, 2005

Industry Group	Unauthorized Workers (in Industry)
Private Households	21%
Food Manufacturing	14%
Agriculture	13%
Furniture Manufacturing	13%
Construction	12%
Textile, Apparel, and Leather Manufacturing	12%
Food Services	12%
Administrative and Support Services	11%
Accommodation	10%

Source: Jeffrey S. Passel, The Size and Characteristics of the Unauthorized Migrant Population in the U.S., Pew Hispanic Center, March 7, 2006.

In a separate Pew Hispanic Center study, Philip Martin, an agricultural labor economist, estimated that there were 1.2 million unauthorized agricultural workers in crop and livestock production in 2002. This figure represented 47% of an estimated total hired farm work force of 2.5 million.[26]

Supporters of a large-scale guest worker program contend that such a program would help reduce unauthorized immigration by providing a legal alternative for prospective foreign workers. Critics reject this reasoning and instead maintain that a guest worker program would likely exacerbate the problem of illegal immigration; they argue, for example, that many guest workers would fail to leave the country at the end of their authorized period of stay.

LEGISLATION IN THE 105TH-107TH CONGRESSES

Major guest worker legislation introduced in the 105th, 106th, and 107th Congresses was limited to the H-2A program.[27] No major nonagricultural guest worker bills were offered.[28] In the 105th Congress, for example, a Senate-approved amendment to S. 2260, an FY1999 Departments of Commerce, Justice, and State Appropriations bill, would have replaced the existing labor certification process with a new set of procedures for importing H-2A workers. It would have established a system of agricultural worker registries containing the names of eligible U.S. agricultural workers. Employers interested in importing H-2A workers would first have applied to DOL for the referral of U.S. workers through a registry search. If a sufficient number of workers were not found, the employer would have been allowed to import H-2A workers to cover the shortfall. The Senate measure also would have changed wage and other requirements. The provision was not enacted.

Provisions to establish a system of worker registries and to change existing H-2A-related requirements were likewise included in two H-2A reform proposals introduced in the 106th Congress (S. 1814/H.R. 4056[29] and H.R. 4548). In addition, S. 1814/H.R. 4056 would have established a two-stage legalization program, under which farm workers satisfying specified work requirements could have obtained temporary resident status and then legal permanent resident (LPR) status. Although formal congressional consideration was limited to a Senate Immigration Subcommittee hearing on S. 1814, S. 1814/H.R. 4056 became the basis of a bipartisan compromise on foreign agricultural workers. That agreement, however, fell apart at the end of the 106th Congress. H.R. 4548, the other reform bill before the 106th Congress, differed from S. 1814/H.R. 4056 in that it sought to establish a pilot H-2C alien agricultural worker program to supplement, rather than replace, the H-2A program. H.R. 4548 also did not include a legalization program. H.R. 4548 was reported by the House Judiciary Committee in October 2000, but saw no further action.

Like S. 1814/H.R. 4056 in the 106th Congress, key bills before the 107th Congress coupled significant H-2A reform with legalization. S. 1161 and S. 1313/H.R. 2736 would have streamlined the process of importing H-2A workers, particularly for jobs covered by collective bargaining agreements. With respect to legalization, both proposals would have allowed foreign agricultural workers who met specified work requirements to adjust to LPR status through a two-stage process like that in S. 1814/H.R. 4056. As detailed below, the requirements for adjustment of status in S. 1313/H.R. 2736 differed from those in S. 1161, with the latter being more stringent. Among the other major differences between the proposals, S. 1161 would have eased existing wage requirements, while S. 1313/H.R. 2736 would have mandated a study of the wage issue. No action beyond committee referral occurred on either proposal.

LEGISLATION IN THE 108TH CONGRESS

Bills to reform the H-2A program, the H-2B program, and the "H" visa category generally, as well as bills to establish new guest worker programs, were introduced in the 108th Congress. Some of these bills would have enabled certain workers to obtain LPR status. No action beyond committee referral occurred on any of the bills.

Congressional committees held related hearings during the 108th Congress. The House Agriculture Committee held a hearing on the potential impact of recent guest worker proposals on the agricultural sector, and the House Judiciary Committee's Subcommittee on Immigration, Border Security, and Claims held a hearing on the impact of guest workers on U.S. workers. In the Senate, the Judiciary Committee's Subcommittee on Immigration, Border Security, and Citizenship held hearings on evaluating a guest worker proposal and on border security under a guest worker program.

S. 1645/H.R. 3142 and S. 2823

The Agricultural Job Opportunity, Benefits, and Security Act of 2003 (AgJOBS bill; S. 1645/H.R. 3142) would have overhauled the H-2A agricultural worker program. It was introduced, respectively, by Senator Craig for himself and a bipartisan group of cosponsors and by Representative Cannon for himself and Representative Berman. Like the major H-2A reform bills before the 107th Congress, S. 1645/H.R. 3142 would have streamlined the process of importing H-

2A workers, particularly for jobs covered by collective bargaining agreements. Under S. 1645/H.R. 3142, prospective H-2A employers would have had to file applications with DOL containing certain assurances. In the case of a job covered by a collective bargaining agreement, the employer would have had to assure, among other things, that there was an applicable union contract and that the bargaining representatives of the employer's employees had been notified of the filing of the application for H-2A workers. An employer interested in filling a job not covered by a collective bargaining agreement would have been subject to a longer list of required assurances. Among these, the employer would have had to assure that he or she would take specified steps to recruit U.S. workers and would provide workers with required benefits, wages, and working conditions. Both groups of employers would have had to assure that the job was temporary or seasonal and that the employer would offer the job to any equally qualified, available U.S. worker who applied. Unless an employer's application was incomplete or obviously inaccurate, DOL would have certified within seven days of the filing date that the employer had filed the required application.

S. 1645/H.R. 3142 further proposed to make changes to the H-2A program's requirements regarding minimum benefits, wages, and working conditions. Among these proposed changes, the adverse effect wage rate (discussed above) would have remained at the January 2003 level for three years after the date of enactment, and employers would have been permitted to provide housing allowances, in lieu of housing, to their workers if the governor of the relevant state certified that adequate housing was available.

Under S. 1645/H.R. 3142, an H-2A worker's initial period of employment could not have exceeded 10 months. The worker's stay could have been extended in increments of up to 10 months each, but the worker's total continuous period of stay, including any extensions, could not have exceeded three years.

In addition to these H-2A reform provisions, S. 1645/H.R. 3142 would have established a two-stage legalization program for agricultural workers. To obtain temporary resident status, the alien worker would have had to establish that he or she performed at least 575 hours, or 100 work days, of agricultural employment in the United States during 12 consecutive months in the 18-month period ending on August 31, 2003, and meet other requirements. To be eligible to adjust to LPR status, the alien would have had to perform at least 2,060 hours, or 360 work days, of agricultural work in the United States between September 1, 2003, and August 31, 2009, and meet other requirements. Existing numerical limits under the INA would not have applied to adjustments of status under the bill.[30]

On September 21, 2004, Senator Craig introduced a modified version of S. 1645 for himself and Senator Kennedy. The revised bill, S. 2823, was very similar to S. 1645, but there were substantive differences in the two bills' legalization provisions. Among these differences, S. 2823 contained a new provision stating that aliens acquiring temporary resident status under the bill would not be eligible for certain federal public benefits until five years after they obtained permanent resident status.[31]

H.R. 3604

Like S. 1645/H.R. 3142, the Temporary Agricultural Labor Reform Act of 2003 (H.R. 3604) proposed to overhaul the H-2A agricultural worker program. It was introduced by Representative Goodlatte for himself and more than 30 co-sponsors. H.R. 3604 would have streamlined the process of importing H-2A workers. Prospective H-2A employers would have had to file applications with DOL containing certain assurances, including that the job was temporary or seasonal; the employer would provide workers with required benefits, wages, and working conditions; the employer had made positive efforts to recruit U.S. workers; and the employer would offer the job to any equally qualified, available U.S. worker who applies. Unless an employer's application was incomplete or obviously inaccurate, DOL would have certified within seven days of the filing date that the employer had filed the required application.

H.R. 3604 would have made changes to current H-2A requirements regarding minimum benefits, wages, and working conditions. Under H.R. 3604, H-2A employers would have had to pay workers the higher of the prevailing wage rate or the applicable state minimum wage; they would not have been subject to the adverse effect wage rate (discussed above). With respect to housing, employers could have provided housing allowances, in lieu of housing, to their workers if the governor of the relevant state certified that adequate housing was available.

Under H.R. 3604, an H-2A worker's initial period of employment could not have exceeded 10 months. The worker's stay could have been extended in increments of up to 10 months each, but the worker's total continuous period of stay, including any extensions, could not have exceeded two years. H.R. 3604 would not have established a mechanism for agricultural workers to obtain LPR status.

S. 2185

Another H-2A reform bill, introduced by Senator Chambliss, was the Temporary Agricultural Work Reform Act of 2004 (S. 2185). It was similar, but not identical, to H.R. 3604. S. 2185 would have streamlined the process of importing H-2A workers. Prospective H-2A employers would have had to file applications with DOL containing certain assurances, including that the job was temporary or seasonal; the employer would provide workers with required benefits, wages, and working conditions; the employer had attempted to recruit U.S. workers using the state workforce agency; and the employer would offer the job to any equally qualified, available U.S. worker who applied. Unless an employer's application was incomplete or obviously inaccurate, DOL would have certified within 15 days of the filing date that the employer had filed the required application.

S. 2185 proposed to change current H-2A requirements concerning minimum benefits, wages, and working conditions. Under S. 2185, H-2A employers would have had to pay workers the higher of the prevailing wage rate or the applicable state minimum wage. In lieu of offering housing, they could have provided housing allowances if the governor of the relevant state certified that adequate housing was available.

S. 2185 did not contain provisions regarding the period of admission, extension of stay, or maximum period of stay of H-2A workers. It also would not have established a mechanism for agricultural workers to obtain LPR status.

S. 2010

The Immigration Reform Act of 2004: Strengthening America's National Security, Economy, and Families (S. 2010), introduced by Senator Hagel for himself and Senator Daschle, would have reformed the H-2B nonimmigrant visa. The bill would have eliminated the current restriction that H-2B workers can perform only temporary service or labor, and instead would have required that they perform "short-term service or labor, lasting not more than 9 months." S. 2010 also proposed a new H-2C visa for temporary workers coming to perform "labor or services, other than those occupation classifications" covered under the H-2A, H-2B, or specified high-skilled visa categories, if qualified U.S. workers cannot be found.

Both the H-2B and H-2C categories would have been numerically limited. In each of the five fiscal years following issuance of final implementing regulations, the H-2B program would have been capped at 100,000. The cap would have then reverted back to the current 66,000 level. The H-2C program would have been capped at 250,000 in each of the five fiscal years following issuance of final implementing regulations. After these five years, the H-2C program would have terminated.

S. 2010 would have subjected both the H-2B and H-2C programs to a broad set of requirements covering recruitment, application procedures, and worker protections, among other issues. Prior to filing an application with DOL for H-2B or H-2C workers, prospective employers would have had to take specified steps to recruit U.S. workers, including posting the job on DOL's "America's Job Bank" and with local job banks, and would have had to offer the job to any qualified, available U.S. worker who applies. In the application to DOL, the employer would have had to attest to various items. Among these are that the employer was offering wages to H-2B or H-2C workers that are the greater of the prevailing wage rate or the actual wage paid by the employer to other similarly employed and qualified workers, and would abide by all applicable laws and regulations relating to the rights of workers to organize. DOL would have reviewed the application and required documentation for completeness and accuracy, and issued a determination not later than 21 days after the filing date.

The initial period of admission for an H-2B worker could not have exceeded nine months in a one-year period. An H-2B worker's total period of admission could not have exceeded 36 months in a four-year period. The initial period of admission for an H-2C worker could not have exceeded two years and could have been extended for an additional period of up to two years. An H-2C worker's total period of admission could not have exceeded four years.

S. 2010 would have enabled H-2B and H-2C nonimmigrants to obtain LPR status. Employment-based *immigrant* visas would have been made available to these nonimmigrants without regard to existing numerical limits under the INA. An employment-based petition could have been filed by an employer or any collective bargaining agent of the alien, or after the alien had been employed in H-2B or H-2C status for at least three years, by the alien. In addition, S. 2010 would have established a legalization program for certain unauthorized aliens in the United States.

S. 2381/H.R. 4262

The Safe, Orderly, Legal Visas and Enforcement Act of 2004 (S. 2381/H.R. 4262) was introduced, respectively, by Senator Kennedy for himself and Senators

Feingold and Clinton and by Representative Gutierrez for himself and a group of cosponsors. Known as the "S.O.L.V.E. Act," the measure would have reformed the H-2B nonimmigrant visa. It would have eliminated the current restriction that H-2B workers can perform only temporary service or labor, and instead would have required that they perform "short-term service or labor, lasting not more than 9 months." S. 2381/H.R. 4262 also proposed a new H-ID visa for temporary workers coming to perform "labor or services, other than those occupation classifications" covered under the H-2A or specified high-skilled visa categories, if qualified U.S. workers cannot be found.

Both the H-2B and H-1D categories would have been numerically limited. The H-2B program would have been capped at 100,000 annually, an increase from the current annual limit of 66,000. The H-1D program would have been capped at 250,000 annually.

S. 2381/H.R. 4262 would have subjected both the H-2B and H-1D programs to a broad set of requirements covering recruitment, application procedures, and worker protections, among other issues. Prior to filing an application with DOL for H-2B or H-1D workers, prospective employers would have had to take specified steps to recruit U.S. workers, including posting the job on DOL's "America's Job Bank" and with local job banks, and would have had to offer the job to any qualified, available U.S. worker who applied. In the application to DOL, the employer would have had to attest to various items. Among these are that the employer was offering to H-2B or H-1D workers the prevailing wage, to be determined as specified in the bill. The employer also would have had to abide by all applicable laws and regulations relating to the rights of workers to organize. DOL would have reviewed the application and required documentation for completeness and accuracy, and issued a determination not later than 10 working days after the filing date.

The initial period of admission for an H-2B worker could not have exceeded nine months in a one-year period. An H-2B worker's total period of admission could not have exceeded 40 months in the aggregate. The initial period of admission for an H-1D worker could not have exceeded two years and could be extended for two additional periods of up to two years each. An H-1D worker's total period of admission could not have exceeded six years.

S. 2381/H.R. 4262 would have enabled H-2B and H-1D nonimmigrants to obtain LPR status. Employment-based *immigrant* visas would have been made available to these nonimmigrants without numerical limitation. An employment-based petition could have been filed by an employer, or after the alien has been employed in H-2B or H-1D status for at least two years, by the alien. In addition,

S. 2381/H.R. 4262 would have established a legalization program for certain unauthorized aliens in the United States.

H.R. 3534

The Border Enforcement and Revolving Employment to Assist Laborers Act of 2003 (H.R. 3534), introduced by Representative Tancredo for himself and several cosponsors, proposed to amend the INA's "H" visa category generally. It would have eliminated the current subcategories, including the H-2A and H-2B visas, and replaced them with a single category covering aliens coming temporarily to the United States to perform skilled or unskilled work if qualified U.S. workers were not available.

An employer interested in importing "H" workers would have filed an application with DOL. Prior to doing so, the employer would have been required to post a job announcement on an Internet-based job bank the bill would have directed DOL to create. Among other requirements of the program, the employer would have had to offer wages at least equal to the prevailing wage rate and would have had to provide "H" workers with health insurance.

H nonmimmigrants could have only been admitted from abroad. They would have applied to be added to a database of workers and would have remained in their home countries until an approved employer wanted to hire them. Their period of authorized admission could not have exceeded 365 days in a two-year period. After the two-year period, H nonimmigrant visas could have been renewed. H nonimmigrants would not have been permitted to change or adjust to any other nonimmigrant or immigrant status.

Under H.R. 3534, however, the proposed guest worker program would not have been implemented until the Secretary of Homeland Security, in consultation with the Attorney General and the Secretary of State, made certain certifications to Congress. These included that all noncitizens legally in the United States and all aliens authorized to enter the country had been issued biometric, machine-readable travel or entry documents, and that the number of aliens who overstay nonimmigrant visas, but were not removed from the United States, was less than 5,000.

S. 1387

The Border Security and Immigration Reform Act of 2003 (S. 1387), introduced by Senator Cornyn, would have authorized new temporary worker programs under the INA for seasonal and nonseasonal workers. S. 1387 would have established a new "W" nonimmigrant visa category for these workers, which would not have been subject to numerical limits. The W-1 visa would have covered seasonal workers, and the W-2 visa would have covered nonseasonal workers. Under the proposal, the Secretary of Homeland Security and the Secretary of State would have jointly established and administered guest worker programs with foreign countries that enter into agreements with the United States. The bill would have directed the Secretary of Homeland Security, in cooperation with the Secretary of State and the participating foreign governments, to establish a database to monitor guest workers' entry into and exit from the United States and to track employer compliance.

In order to import workers through the new programs, employers would have had to file an application with DOL. As part of the application, the employer would have had to request an attestation from DOL that there were not sufficient U.S. workers who were qualified and available to perform the work, and that the hiring of alien workers would not adversely affect the wages and working conditions of similarly employed U.S. workers. The employer also would have needed to provide various assurances in the application, including that the employer would offer the job to any equally qualified, available U.S. worker who applied; would advertise the job opening in a local publication; and would pay workers at least the higher of the federal or applicable state minimum wage. Unless an employer's application was incomplete or obviously inaccurate, DOL would have certified within 14 days of the filing date that the application had been filed. Beginning 12 months after enactment, employers would have been subject to increased penalties for knowingly employing unauthorized aliens.

The authorized period of stay for a W-1 seasonal worker could not have exceeded 270 days per year. Such a worker could have reapplied for admission to the United States each year. The initial authorized period of stay for a W-2 non-seasonal worker could not have exceeded one year, but could have been extended in increments of up to one year each; a W-2 worker's total period of stay could not have exceeded three consecutive years. Unauthorized workers in the United States would have had 12 months from enactment to apply for the program.

Among the other provisions, the bill would have created investment accounts for the guest workers, into which the Social Security taxes paid by them and by their employers on their behalf would have been deposited. The investment accounts would have been the sole property of the guest workers. In most cases, however, distributions of account funds could have been made only after the workers permanently left the guest worker program and returned to their home countries.

Under S. 1387, guest workers could have applied for U.S. legal permanent residency only once they returned to their home countries. Their applications would have been evaluated based on a point system to be established by the Secretary of Homeland Security. The bill did not propose a legalization mechanism for guest workers outside of existing channels, and according to Senator Cornyn's office, guest workers would have had to meet all the relevant requirements under current law.[32]

S. 1461/H.R. 2899

The Border Security and Immigration Improvement Act (S. 1461/H.R. 2899), introduced, respectively, by Senator McCain and by Representative Kolbe for himself and Representative Flake, would have established two new temporary worker visas under the INA — the H-4A and H-4B visas. It would have placed no limit on the number of H-4A or H-4B visas that could have been issued.

The H-4A visa would have covered aliens coming to the United States to perform temporary full-time employment. An employer interested in importing H-4A workers would have had to file a petition with DHS. DHS could only have approved the petition once it determined that the employer had satisfied recruitment requirements, including advertising the job opportunity to U.S. workers on an electronic job registry established by DOL and offering the job to any equally qualified U.S. worker who applied through the registry. The employer also would have had to attest in the petition that he or she would use the employment eligibility confirmation system established by the bill to verify the alien workers' identity and employment authorization; would provide the alien workers with the same benefits, wages, and working conditions as other similarly employed workers; and did not and would not displace U.S. workers during a specified 180-day period. Aliens granted H-4A status would have been issued machine-readable, tamper-resistant visas and other documents containing biometric identifiers.

An H-4A worker's initial authorized period of stay would have been three years, and could have been extended for an additional three years. S. 1461/H.R. 2899 also would have enabled H-4A nonimmigrants to adjust to LPR status. Petitions for employment-based *immigrant* visas could have been filed by an H-

4A worker's employer, or by the H-4A worker, if he or she had maintained H-4A status for at least three years. Employment-based immigrant visas would have been made available to H-4A workers adjusting status without numerical limitation.

The H-4B visa established by the bill would have covered aliens unlawfully present and employed in the United States since before August 1, 2003. An H-4B alien's authorized period of stay would have been three years. The alien could have applied to change to H-4A status or another nonimmigrant or immigrant category, but such a change of status could not have taken place until the end of the three years. H-4B employers would have been required to use the employment eligibility confirmation system mentioned above and to comply with specified requirements applicable to H-4A employers, including the provision of benefits, wages, and working conditions to H-4B workers equal to those provided to other similarly employed workers.

H.R. 3651

The Alien Accountability Act (H.R. 3651), introduced by Representative Issa, would have authorized a new "W" nonimmigrant visa category under the INA for unauthorized aliens. The category would have covered aliens unlawfully present in the United States on December 8, 2003, as well as aliens residing in foreign contiguous territory who were habitually unlawfully present in the United States during the six-month period ending on December 8, 2003. In order to have been eligible for W status, the alien would first have had to register with DHS. Employment would not have been a strict requirement for W status, but the alien would have had to demonstrate an adequate means of financial support. The new category would have sunset six years after the first alien was granted W status.

The initial period of authorized admission of a W nonimmigrant would have been one year and could have been renewed up to five times in one-year increments. H.R. 3651 would not have established a special mechanism for W nonimmigrants to adjust to LPR status. It, however, would not have precluded them from doing so if they satisfied the applicable requirements under current law.

LEGISLATION IN THE 109TH CONGRESS

Bills have been introduced in the 109th Congress to reform the H-2A and H-2B programs, to reform the "H" visa category, and to establish new temporary worker visas. An amendment based on one of the H-2B bills (S. 352/H.R. 793) was enacted as part of the FY2005 Emergency Supplemental Appropriations Act for Defense, the Global War on Terror, and Tsunami Relief (P.L. 109-13). As discussed below, the immigration reform bill approved by the Senate Judiciary Committee on March 27, 2006, would reform the H-2A program and would establish a new guest worker program for nonagricultural workers. During consideration of the "Border Protection, Antiterrorism, and Illegal Immigration Control Act of 2005" (H.R. 4437) by the House Judiciary Committee and on the House floor, efforts were made to add guest worker programs and language expressing support for a guest worker program, but they were unsuccessful. H.R. 4437, as passed by the House, does not contain any guest worker provisions.

The 109th Congress also has held a number of hearings on immigration issues relevant to a guest worker program. The House Judiciary Committee's Subcommittee on Immigration, Border Security, and Claims has held hearings on employment eligibility verification and work site enforcement. The Senate Judiciary Committee's Subcommittee on Immigration, Border Security, and Citizenship has held hearings on immigration reform issues, including the establishment of a new guest worker program. The full Senate Judiciary Committee has held two hearings on comprehensive immigration reform, at which two major reform proposals (S. 1033/H.R. 2330 and S. 1438) were discussed.

S. 352/H.R. 793

The Save Our Small and Seasonal Businesses Act (S. 352/H.R. 793),[33] introduced respectively by Senator Mikulski and Representative Gilchrest for themselves and bipartisan groups of cosponsors, proposed to revise the H-2B program. During Senate consideration of the FY2005 Emergency Supplemental Appropriations bill (H.R. 1268) in April 2005, Senator Mikulski offered a floor amendment based on S. 352/H.R. 793. On April 19, 2005, the Senate adopted the Mikulski Amendment, as modified, by a vote of 94 to 6, and the amendment was included in the enacted measure (P.L. 109-13) as Division B, Title IV.

The H-2B title of P.L. 109-13 contains a provision that keeps aliens who have been counted toward the H-2B cap in any of the past three years from being counted again. This provision expires at the end of FY2006. The title also caps at

33,000 the number of H-2B slots available during the first six months of a fiscal year. In addition, it requires DHS to submit specified information to Congress on the H-2B program on a regular basis, imposes a new fraud-prevention and detection fee on H-2B employers, and authorizes DHS to impose additional penalties on H-2B employers in certain circumstances.

Specter Substitute to S. 2454

In March 2006, the Senate Judiciary Committee considered an immigration measure by Chairman Specter, known as the Chairman's mark. This measure, as amended and approved by the Committee, proposed to reform the H-2A program and establish a new guest worker program for nonagricultural workers. On March 30, 2006, during Senate floor debate on the Securing America's Borders Act (S. 2454), introduced by Senator Frist, Senator Specter proposed a substitute amendment based on the Judiciary Committee-approved bill. On April 6, 2006, the Senate rejected a motion, by a vote of 39 to 60, to invoke cloture (and thereby initiate post-cloture procedures to eventually move to a vote) on the Specter substitute.

Title VI, Subtitle B, of the Specter substitute contains provisions on agricultural workers. These provisions, which are similar to those in the Agricultural Job Opportunities, Benefits, and Security Act of 2005 (S. 359/H.R. 884), known as AgJOBS, were offered as an amendment by Senator Feinstein to the Chairman's mark during the Senate Judiciary Committee mark-up. Like S. 359/H.R. 884, Title VI of the Specter substitute would streamline the process of importing H-2A workers, particularly for jobs covered by collective bargaining agreements. Prospective H-2A employers would have to file applications with DOL containing certain assurances. In the case of a job covered by a collective bargaining agreement, the employer would have to assure, among other things, that there is an applicable union contract and that the bargaining representatives of the employer's employees have been notified of the filing of the application for H-2A workers. An employer interested in filling a job not covered by a collective bargaining agreement would be subject to a longer list of required assurances. Among these, the employer would have to assure that he or she will take specified steps to recruit U.S. workers and will provide workers with required benefits, wages, and working conditions. Both groups of employers would have to assure that the job is temporary or seasonal and that the employer will offer the job to any equally qualified, available U.S. worker who applies. Unless an employer's application is incomplete or obviously inaccurate, DOL would certify within seven days of the filing date that the employer has filed the required application.

Title VI of the Specter substitute would make changes to the H-2A program's requirements regarding minimum benefits, wages, and working conditions. Among these proposed changes, the adverse effect wage rate (discussed above) would remain at the January 2003 level for three years after the date of enactment, and employers would be permitted to provide housing allowances, in lieu of housing, to their workers if the governor of the relevant state certifies that adequate housing is available. An H-2A worker's initial period of employment could not exceed 10 months. The worker's stay could be extended in increments of up to 10 months each, but the worker's total continuous period of stay, including any extensions, could not exceed three years.

Title VI of the Specter substitute also proposes a legalization program for agricultural workers. This program follows the basic design of the legalization program in S. 359/H.R. 884, but includes different work and other requirements and uses different terminology. Under the program in the Specter substitute, the Secretary of DHS would confer "blue card status" (akin to S. 359/H.R. 884's temporary resident status)[34] on an alien worker who has performed at least 863 hours, or 150 work days, of agricultural employment in the United States during the 24-month period ending on December 31, 2005, and meets other requirements. No more than 1.5 million blue cards could be issued during the five-year period beginning on the date of enactment. To be eligible to adjust to LPR status, the alien in blue card status would have to, among other requirements, perform either at least 575 hours of U.S. agricultural work per year for the five years after enactment, or at least 863 hours of U.S. agricultural work per year for three of the five years after enactment.

Existing numerical limits under the INA would not apply to adjustments of status under the bill.[35]

Title IV, Subtitle A, of the Specter substitute would establish a new H-2C nonagricultural guest worker program. These H-2C provisions represent guest worker language in the Chairman's mark, as subsequently modified, including by an amendment offered by Senator Kennedy during the Senate Judiciary Committee mark-up. The Kennedy amendment, in turn, was based, in part, on guest worker provisions in S. 1033/H.R. 2330, discussed below. The proposed H-2C visa would be capped at 400,000 the first fiscal year. The bill would establish a process for adjusting the cap in subsequent fiscal years based on demand for the visas.

The H-2C visa would cover aliens coming temporarily to the United States to perform temporary labor or services other than the labor or services covered under the H-2A visa or other specified visa categories. A prospective H-2C employer would file a petition with DHS. In the petition the employer would have to attest to various items, including that the employer is offering wages to H-2C workers that are the greater of the prevailing wage rate for the occupational classification in the area of employment or the actual wage paid by the employer to other similarly employed and qualified workers; and that there are not sufficient qualified and available U.S. workers to perform the work. Prior to filing the petition, the prospective employer also would have to make efforts to recruit U.S. workers in accordance with DOL regulations. Under the bill, the Secretary of State could grant an H-2C visa to an alien who demonstrates an intent to perform work covered by the visa. To be eligible for H-2C status, the alien would need to have evidence of employment and meet other requirements.

An H-2C worker's initial authorized period of stay would be three years, and could be extended for an additional three years. H-2C aliens could not change to another nonimmigrant visa category. As in S. 1438 (discussed below), an H-2C alien who failed to depart the United States when required to do so would be ineligible for any immigration relief or benefit, except for specified forms of humanitarian relief. At the same time, H-2C nonimmigrants in the United States could adjust to LPR status. Petitions for employment-based *immigrant* visas could be filed by an H-2C worker's employer or, if the H-2C worker had maintained H-2C status for a total of four years, by the worker.

Under separate provisions in Title VI, Subtitle A, of the bill, the Secretary of DHS would grant "conditional nonimmigrant work authorization and status" to remain in the United States to aliens who were physically present in the country before January 7, 2004; have been employed in the United States since before that date; and meet other requirements. The authorized period of stay of such conditional nonimmigrants would be six years, during which time they could not change to another nonimmigrant or immigrant classification. After the six years, DHS would adjust the status of the alien to that of an LPR if the alien meets specified work and other requirements. Such adjustments of status would not be subject to numerical limits. The status of conditional nonimmigrants could not be adjusted to LPR status, however, until the visa priority dates become current for the petitions for family-based and employment-based immigrant visas pending on the date of enactment.[36]

S. 359/H.R. 884

The Agricultural Job Opportunities, Benefits, and Security Act of 2005 (AgJOBS bill; S. 359/H.R. 884) proposes to overhaul the H-2A agricultural worker program. The bills were introduced, respectively, by Senator Craig and Representative Cannon for themselves and bipartisan groups of cosponsors. S. 359/H.R. 884 is very similar to the AgJOBs bills before the 108th Congress (S. 1645/H.R. 3142, S. 2823). Like these bills, S. 359/H.R. 884 would streamline the process of importing H-2A workers, particularly for jobs covered by collective bargaining agreements. Prospective H-2A employers would have to file applications with DOL containing certain assurances. In the case of a job covered by a collective bargaining agreement, the employer would have to assure, among other things, that there is an applicable union contract and that the bargaining representatives of the employer's employees have been notified of the filing of the application for H-2A workers. An employer interested in filling a job not covered by a collective bargaining agreement would be subject to a longer list of required assurances. Among these, the employer would have to assure that he or she will take specified steps to recruit U.S. workers and will provide workers with required benefits, wages, and working conditions. Both groups of employers would have to assure that the job is temporary or seasonal and that the employer will offer the job to any equally qualified, available U.S. worker who applies. Unless an employer's application is incomplete or obviously inaccurate, DOL would certify within seven days of the filing date that the employer has filed the required application.

S. 359/H.R. 884 would make changes to the H-2A program's requirements regarding minimum benefits, wages, and working conditions. Among these proposed changes, the adverse effect wage rate (discussed above) would remain at the January 2003 level for three years after the date of enactment, and employers would be permitted to provide housing allowances, in lieu of housing, to their workers if the governor of the relevant state certifies that adequate housing is available.

Under S. 359/H.R. 884, an H-2A worker would be admitted for an initial period of employment not exceed 10 months. The worker's stay could be extended in increments of up to 10 months each, but the worker's total continuous period of stay, including any extensions, could not exceed three years.

In addition to these H-2A reform provisions, S. 359/H.R. 884 would establish a two-stage legalization program for agricultural workers. To obtain temporary resident status, the alien worker would have to establish that he or she performed at least 575 hours, or 100 work days, of agricultural employment in the United

States during 12 consecutive months in the 18-month period ending on December 31, 2004, and meet other requirements. To be eligible to adjust to LPR status, the alien would have to perform at least 2,060 hours, or 360 work days, of agricultural work in the United States during the six years following the date of enactment, and meet other requirements. Existing numerical limits under the INA would not apply to adjustments of status under the bills.[37]

H.R. 3857

The Temporary Agricultural Labor Reform Act of 2005 (H.R. 3857), an H-2A reform bill introduced by Representative Goodlatte on behalf of himself and a group of cosponsors, revises a bill that he introduced by the same name in the 108th Congress. H.R. 3857 would streamline the process of importing H-2A workers. Prospective H-2A employers would have to file petitions with DHS containing certain attestations; they would not file applications with DOL as they currently do. They would have to attest that the job is temporary or seasonal; that the employer will provide workers with required benefits, wages, and working conditions; that the employer has made efforts to recruit U.S. workers; and that the employer will offer the job to any equally qualified, available U.S. worker who applies. Unless an employer's application is incomplete or obviously inaccurate, DHS would have to adjudicate the petition within seven days of the filing date.

H.R. 3857 would change current H-2A requirements regarding minimum benefits, wages, and working conditions. Under the bill, H-2A employers would have to pay workers the higher of the prevailing wage rate or the applicable state minimum wage; employers would not be subject to the adverse effect wage rate (discussed above). With respect to housing, employers could provide allowances, in lieu of housing, to their workers if the governor of the relevant state certifies that adequate housing is available.

Under H.R. 3857, an H-2A worker would be admitted for an initial period of employment not exceed 10 months. The worker's stay could be extended in increments of up to 10 months each, but the worker's total continuous period of stay, including any extensions, could not exceed 20 months. H.R. 3857 would not establish a mechanism for agricultural workers to obtain LPR status.

S. 2087

The Agricultural Employment and Workforce Protection Act of 2005 (S. 2087), introduced by Senator Chambliss, would reform the H-2A program. It would eliminate the current limitation that H-2A nonimmigrants perform temporary or seasonal work and would broaden the definition of agricultural labor or services for purposes of the H-2A visa to cover labor or services relating to such activities as dairy, forestry, landscaping, and meat processing. Like S. 359/H.R. 884 and H.R. 3857, S. 2087 proposes to streamline the process of importing H-2A workers. As under H.R. 3857, a prospective H-2A employer would file a petition with DHS containing certain attestations. Among them, the employer would have to attest that the employer will provide workers with required benefits, wages, and working conditions; that the employer has made efforts to recruit U.S. workers; and that the employer will offer the job to any equally qualified, available U.S. worker who applies. Unless the petition is incomplete or obviously inaccurate, DHS would have to approve or deny the petition not later than seven days after the filing date.

Also like S. 359/H.R. 884 and H.R. 3857, S. 2087 would change current H-2A requirements regarding minimum benefits, wages, and working conditions. Under S. 2087, H-2A employers would have to pay workers the higher of the prevailing wage rate or the applicable state minimum wage; employers would not be subject to the adverse effect wage rate (discussed above). As under both S. 359/H.R. 884 and H.R. 3857, employers could provide housing allowances, in lieu of housing, to their workers if the governor of the relevant state certifies that adequate housing is available. Under S. 2087, an H-2A worker would be admitted for an initial period of employment of 11 months. The worker's stay could be extended for up to two consecutive contract periods.

Unlike S. 359/H.R. 884 and H.R. 3857, S. 2087 would establish subcategories of H-2A nonimmigrants. It would define a "Level II H-2A worker" as a nonimmigrant who has been employed as an H-2A worker for at least three years and works in a supervisory capacity. The bill would make provision for an employer of a Level II H-2A worker, who has been employed in such status for not less than five years, to file an application for an employment-based adjustment of status for that worker. Such a Level II H-2A worker could continue to be employed in such status until his or her application was adjudicated. Under the bill, an "H-2AA worker" would be defined as an H-2A worker who participates in the cross-border worker program the bill would establish. These H-2AA workers would be allowed to enter and exit the United States each work day in accordance with DHS regulations.

In addition, the bill would establish a blue card program through which the Secretary of DHS could confer "blue card status" upon an alien, including an unauthorized alien, who has performed at least 1,600 hours of agricultural employment for an employer in the United States in 2005 and meets other requirements. An alien may be granted blue card status for a period of up to two years, at the end of which the alien would have to return to his or her home country. Aliens in blue card status would not be eligible to change to an nonimmigrant status or adjust to LPR status.

S. 278

The Summer Operations and Seasonal Equity Act of 2005 (S. 278), introduced by Senator Collins, would make changes to the numerical limits under the H-2B program. It would require that at least 12,000 of the total number of H-2B slots available annually (currently, 66,000) be made available in each quarter of each fiscal year. It would exempt an alien who has been counted toward the annual H-2B numerical limit within the past three years from being counted again. Both of these provisions would expire at the end of FY2007. S. 278 also would require DHS to submit specified information to Congress on the H-2B program on a regular basis.

H.R. 1587

H.R. 1587, introduced by Representative Tancredo for himself and several cosponsors, would raise the H-2B cap and place new requirements on the H-2B program. It would increase to 131,000 the number of aliens who could be issued H-2B visas or otherwise provided H-2B status annually. Not more than half of these slots, or 65,500, would be available during the first six months of a fiscal year. H.R. 1587 would add new recruitment-related requirements for prospective H-2B employers, and would mandate H-2B employer participation in the Basic Pilot program, an electronic employment eligibility verification system. H.R. 1587 also would impose new requirements on H-2B nonimmigrants. Among them, these aliens could no longer be accompanied by family members.

S. 1918

The Strengthening America's Workforce Act of 2005 (S. 1918), introduced by Senator Hagel, contains guest worker provisions similar to those in the bill he introduced in the 108th Congress. S. 1918 would revise the H-2B visa and eliminate the current restriction that H-2B workers can perform only temporary service or labor. Instead, the bill would require workers to perform "short-term service or labor, lasting not more than nine months." S. 1918 also would establish a new H-2C visa for temporary workers coming to perform "labor or services, other than those occupation classifications" covered under the H-2A, H-2B, or specified high-skilled visa categories. The H-2B visa would be capped at 100,000 annually, and the H-2C visa would be capped at 250,000 annually.

S. 1918 would subject the H-2B and H-2C programs to a broad set of requirements concerning recruitment, application procedures, and worker protections, among other issues. Prior to filing an application with DOL for H-2B or H-2C workers, prospective employers would have to take specified steps to recruit U.S. workers, including authorizing DOL to post the job on a national online job registry called America's Job Bank and on local job banks. Employers also would have to offer the job to any qualified, available U.S. worker who applies. In the application to DOL, the employer would have to attest to various items. Among these are that the employer is offering wages to H-2B or H-2C workers that are the greater of the prevailing wage rate or the actual wage paid by the employer to other similarly employed and qualified workers, and that the employer would abide by all applicable laws and regulations relating to the rights of workers to organize. DOL would review the application for completeness and accuracy and issue a determination not later than 21 days after the filing date.

The initial period of admission for an H-2B worker could not exceed nine months in a one-year period. An H-2B worker's total period of admission could not exceed 36 months in a four-year period. The initial period of admission for an H-2C worker could not exceed two years and could be extended for an additional period of up to two years. An H-2C worker's total period of admission could not exceed four years.

S. 2010 would enable H-2B and H-2C nonimmigrants to obtain LPR status. Employment-based immigrant visas would be made available to nonimmigrants without regard to existing numerical limits under the INA. An employment-based petition could be filed by an alien's employer or collective bargaining agent or by the alien, after the alien has been employed in H-2B or H-2C status for at least three years.

H.R. 3333

The Rewarding Employers that Abide by the Law and Guaranteeing Uniform Enforcement to Stop Terrorism Act of 2005 (H.R. 3333), introduced by Representative Tancredo, contains temporary worker provisions similar to those in the bill he introduced in the 108th Congress. H.R. 3333 would eliminate all the current "H" visa subcategories, including the H-2A and H-2B visas, and replace them with a single "H" visa covering aliens coming temporarily to the United States to perform skilled or unskilled work. There would be no cap on the H visa.

An employer interested in employing H nonimmigrants would have to recruit U.S. workers by posting the job opportunity on America's Job Bank and would have to offer the job to any equally qualified U.S. worker who applies. The employer would have to file an application with DOL containing certain assurances, including that he or she has complied with the recruitment requirements.

Prospective H nonimmigrants, who could only be admitted from abroad, would apply to be included in a database of workers, which DOL would be tasked with establishing and maintaining. Once an employer's application was approved, DOL would provide the employer with a list of aliens from the database who may be able to fill the position. Aliens admitted on H visas could not change to another nonimmigrant status or adjust to LPR status in the United States.

Under H.R. 3333, the new H visa program could not be implemented until the Secretary of Homeland Security makes certain certifications to Congress, including that a congressionally mandated automated entry-exit system is fully operational[38] and that at least 80% of aliens who overstay their nonimmigrants visas are removed within one year of overstaying.

S. 1033/H.R. 2330

The Secure America and Orderly Immigration Act (S. 1033/H.R. 2330) was introduced, respectively, by Senator McCain and Representative Kolbe for themselves and bipartisan groups of cosponsors. It was discussed at the Senate Judiciary Committee hearings on comprehensive immigration reform held in July 2005 and October 2005. Its guest worker and legalization provisions are similar in some respects to provisions in bills from the 108th Congress, including S. 1461/H.R. 2899, S. 2010, and S. 2381/H.R. 4262. S. 1033/H.R. 2330 would establish two new temporary worker visas under the INA — the H-5A and H-5B visas. It would cap the H-5A visa initially at 400,000, and would establish a process for adjusting the cap in subsequent fiscal years based on demand for the visas. It would place no cap on the H-5B visa.

The H-5A visa would cover aliens coming temporarily to the United States *initially* to perform labor or services "other than those occupational classifications" covered under the H-2A or specified high-skilled visa categories. Prospective H-5A nonimmigrants would file visa applications on their own behalf. Employers would not file petitions with DHS for them, as they currently do to employ other nonimmigrant workers. Under S. 1033/H.R. 2330, the Secretary of State may grant an H-5A visa to an alien who demonstrates an intent to perform work covered by the visa. To be eligible for H-5A status, the alien would need to have evidence of employment and meet other requirements. Before hiring a prospective H-5A worker, an employer would have to post the job opportunity on a DOL electronic job registry to recruit U.S. workers. H-5A employers also would be required to comply with all applicable federal, state, and local laws, and to use an employment eligibility confirmation system, to be established by the Social Security Administration, to verify the employment eligibility of newly hired H-5A workers.

An H-5A worker's initial authorized period of stay would be three years, and could be extended for an additional three years. Under S. 1033/H.R. 2330, H-5A nonimmigrants in the United States could adjust to LPR status. Petitions for employment-based *immigrant* visas could be filed by an H-5A worker's employer or, if the H-5A worker had maintained H-5A status for a total of four years, by the worker.

The H-5B visa established by the bill would cover aliens present and employed in the United States since before May 12, 2005. Aliens lawfully present in the United States as nonimmigrants on that date would not be eligible for H-5B status. An H-5B alien's authorized period of stay would be six years. At the end of that six-year period, the alien could apply to adjust to LPR status, subject to various requirements. Such adjustments of status would not be subject to numerical limitations.

S. 1438

The Comprehensive Enforcement and Immigration Reform Act of 2005 (S. 1438) was introduced by Senator Cornyn for himself and Senator Kyl. Like S. 1033/H.R. 2330, it was discussed at the Senate Judiciary Committee hearings on comprehensive immigration reform held in July 2005 and October 2005. It would establish a new "W" temporary worker visa under the INA. S. 1438 would not place a cap on the W visa, but would authorize DOL to do so in the future based on the recommendations of a task force the bill would establish. In addition, S. 1438 would amend the INA to authorize DHS to grant a new status — Deferred Mandatory Departure (DMD) status — to certain unauthorized aliens in the United States. It would place no limit on the number of aliens who could receive that status.

The W visa would cover aliens coming temporarily to the United States to perform temporary labor or service other than that covered under the H-2A or specified high-skilled visa categories. S. 1438 would repeal the H-2B visa category. Prospective W nonimmigrants would file applications on their own behalf. Employers would not file petitions with DHS on behalf of W workers, as they currently do to employ other nonimmigrant workers. Under S. 1438, the Secretary of State may grant a W visa to an alien who demonstrates an intent to perform eligible work. To be eligible for W status, the alien would need to have evidence of employment, among other requirements. An employer interested in hiring a W nonimmigrant would have to apply for authorization to do so through an Alien Employment Management System to be established by DHS. Before an employer could be granted such authorization, he or she would have to post the position on a DOL electronic job registry and offer the position to any equally qualified U.S. worker who applied. S. 1438 would make it mandatory for all employers, including W employers, to verify the employment eligibility of new hires through an electronic system. Current electronic employment eligibility verification is conducted through the largely voluntary basic pilot program.

A W nonimmigrant's authorized period of stay would be two years, and could *not* be extended. After residing in his or her home country for one year, however, an alien could be readmitted to the United States in W status. An alien's total period of admission as a W nonimmigrant could not exceed six years. These stay limitations would not apply to aliens who spend less than six months a year in W status, or who commute to the United States to work in W status but reside outside the country. S. 1438 would make W nonimmigrants ineligible to change to another nonimmigrant status and would not provide them with any special mechanism to obtain LPR status. Furthermore, a W nonimmigrant who did not depart the United States when required to do so would be ineligible for any immigration benefit or relief, except for specified forms of humanitarian relief.

Aliens present in the United States since July 20, 2004, and employed since before July 20, 2005, could apply to DHS for Deferred Mandatory Departure (DMD) status. Aliens lawfully present in the United States as nonimmigrants would not be eligible. DHS could grant an alien DMD status for a period of up to five years. Employers interested in employing aliens granted DMD status would have to apply for authorization through the Alien Employment Management System mentioned above. Aliens in DMD status could not apply to change to a nonimmigrant status or, unless otherwise eligible under INA §245(i), to adjust to LPR status.[39] Aliens who comply with the terms of DMD status and depart prior to its expiration date would not be subject to the INA provision that bars previously unlawfully present aliens from being admitted to the United States for 3 or 10 years, depending on the length of their unlawful stay.[40] If otherwise eligible, these aliens could immediately seek admission as nonimmigrants or immigrants. However, they would not receive any special consideration for admission. Aliens granted DMD status who failed to depart prior to the expiration of that status would be ineligible for any immigration benefit or relief, except for specified forms of humanitarian relief, for 10 years.

H.R. 4065

The Temporary Worker Registration and Visa Act of 2005 (H.R. 4065), introduced by Representative Osborne, would establish a process for registering aliens who have been continuously unlawfully present and employed in the United States since January 1, 2005. Eligible aliens would apply for this registration, which would be valid for six months. Registered aliens would be given work authorization and would be eligible for a new "W" temporary worker visa established by the bill. To obtain a W visa, a registered alien would have to apply at a consular office in his or her home country during a six-month registration period. H.R. 4065 would place no numerical limit on the W visa.

The initial period of authorized admission for a W nonimmigrant would be three years and could be extended in three year increments without limit. H.R. 4065 would require that W nonimmigrants be continuously employed but would place no restriction on the type of work they could perform. W nonimmigrants would not be prohibited from changing to another nonimmigrant classification or adjusting to LPR status. H.R. 4065, however, would make no special provision enabling them to do so.

BUSH ADMINISTRATION PROPOSAL

On January 7, 2004, President Bush outlined an immigration reform proposal, at the center of which is a new temporary worker program.[41] The President featured his proposal in the 2004 and 2005 State of the Union addresses.

According to the White House fact sheet on the proposal, the temporary worker program is intended "to match willing foreign workers with willing U.S. employers when no Americans can be found to fill the jobs." The program, which would grant participants legal temporary status, would initially be open to both foreign workers abroad and unauthorized aliens within the United States. At some future date, however, it would be restricted to aliens outside the country. The temporary workers' authorized period of stay would be three years and would be renewable for an unspecified period of time. Temporary workers would be able to travel back and forth between their home countries and the United States, and, as stated in the background briefing for reporters, would "enjoy the same protections that American workers have with respect to wages and employment rights." The proposal also calls for increased workplace enforcement of immigration laws.

The proposal would not establish a special mechanism for participants in the temporary worker program to obtain LPR status. According to the fact sheet, the program "should not permit undocumented workers to gain an advantage over those who have followed the rules." Temporary workers would be expected to return to their home countries at the end of their authorized period of stay, and the Administration favors providing them with economic incentives to do so. As stated in the fact sheet:

> The U.S. will work with other countries to allow aliens working in the U.S. to receive credit in their nations' retirement systems and will support the creation of tax-preferred savings accounts they can collect when they return to their native countries.

Although it does not include a permanent legalization mechanism, the program would not prohibit temporary workers from applying for legal permanent residency under existing immigration law.

According to the Administration, the proposed temporary worker program should support efforts to improve homeland security by controlling the U.S. borders. The fact sheet states that "the program should link to efforts to control our border through agreements with countries whose nationals participate in the program," but does not elaborate further on this issue.

At the October 2005 Senate Judiciary Committee hearing on comprehensive immigration reform, Labor Secretary Elaine Chao reiterated the Administration's support for the immigration reform ideas that President Bush outlined in January 2004.[42] She did not offer a detailed legislative proposal and did not take a position on any of the pending immigration reform bills. Secretary Chao described the Administration's plan as having three components — border security, interior enforcement, and a temporary worker program — and not allowing "amnesty." She maintained that "an improved temporary worker program will enhance border security and interior enforcement by providing a workable and enforceable process for hiring foreign workers."

Both in her written testimony and in responses to Senators' questions, Secretary Chao made some general statements about the type of temporary worker program the Administration favors. She made reference to "streamlining the process so that willing workers can efficiently be matched with employers ... [when] there are no willing U.S. workers." Although she did not describe this streamlined process, she did state that private for-profit or nonprofit organizations could play a role in matching employers and workers. She also explained that under the President's temporary worker program, prospective employers would be subject to labor certification, as they currently are under the H-2A and H-2B programs. In describing how the President's program would overcome problems in existing guest worker programs, Secretary Chao referred generally to "a technologically advanced new system" through which "workers will have visa documentation that clearly establishes their eligibility to work" and "employers will have access to a verification system that enables them to quickly check the eligibility and verify the identity of potential employees."

POLICY CONSIDERATIONS

Issues raised in connection with temporary worker programs — such as U.S. economic development, Mexican economic development, law enforcement, and worker protections — coupled with the U.S. experience with the H-2A and H-2B programs, suggest policy issues likely to arise in the evaluation of guest worker proposals.

Comparison of Program Requirements

A new guest worker program could include agricultural workers or nonagricultural workers or both. It could replace or supplement one or both of the existing H-2A and H-2B programs. The assessment of any proposed program would likely include a comparison of the requirements of the proposed and existing programs, especially in the case of a new program covering both agricultural and nonagricultural workers since current H-2A and H-2B requirements vary considerably.

The area of wages provides an example. Under the H-2B program, employers must pay their workers at least the prevailing wage rate. Employers importing agricultural workers through the H-2A program are subject to potentially higher wage requirements. As explained above, they must pay their workers the highest of the minimum wage, the prevailing wage rate, or the AEWR. Therefore, a new guest worker program that covered both agricultural and nonagricultural workers and included a unified wage requirement would represent a change in existing wage requirements for employers.

Eligible Population

A guest worker program could be limited to aliens within the country (many of whom presumably would be unauthorized aliens) or to aliens outside the country or could include both groups. The possible participation of illegal aliens in a guest worker program is controversial. Some parties would likely see their inclusion as rewarding lawbreakers and encouraging future unauthorized immigration, especially if the program enabled some participants to obtain LPR status. The option of excluding unauthorized aliens has raised another set of concerns. Some observers maintain that a large guest worker program limited to new workers could leave unauthorized aliens in the United States particularly vulnerable to exploitation by unscrupulous employers. More generally, many who view a guest worker program as a means of addressing the unauthorized alien problem see the inclusion of unauthorized aliens as integral to any proposal.

Another eligibility question is whether the program would be limited to nationals of certain countries. The Bush Administration began discussion of a guest worker program with Mexico in 2001 as part of binational migration talks, and some immigration experts maintain that "there are very good reasons for crafting a special immigration relationship with Mexico, given its propinquity, its historical ties and NAFTA."[43] Some immigrant advocacy groups, however, have argued that it would be unfair to single out Mexicans for special treatment, especially if legalization were part of the agreement.[44]

Legalization of Program Participants

The issue of whether to include a legalization or *earned adjustment* program as part of a guest worker proposal is controversial. *Earned adjustment* is the term used to describe legalization programs that require prospective beneficiaries to "earn" LPR status through work and/or other contributions. Some see permanent legalization as an essential element of a guest worker proposal,[45] while others oppose the inclusion of any type of LPR adjustment program. In the current debate, reference is often made to two legalization programs established by the Immigration Reform and Control Act (IRCA) of 1986: (1) a general program for unauthorized aliens who had been continually resident in the United States since before January 1, 1982; and (2) a special agricultural worker (SAW) program for aliens who had worked at least 90 days in seasonal agriculture during a designated year-long period.[46] Approximately 2.7 million individuals have adjusted to LPR status under these programs.[47]

Recent H-2A reform bills suggest a willingness on the part of some policymakers to establish an earned adjustment program, at least for agricultural workers. A key set of questions about any legalization mechanism proposed as part of a guest worker program would concern the proposed legalization process and associated requirements. Major H-2A reform proposals introduced in the 107th Congress (S. 1313/H.R. 2736 and S. 1161), for example, would have established similarly structured earned adjustment programs for agricultural workers. Under both proposals, workers who had performed a requisite amount of agricultural work could have applied for temporary resident status. After satisfying additional work requirements in subsequent years, they could have applied for LPR status. The applicable requirements in the proposals, however, differed significantly. For temporary resident status, S. 1313/H.R. 2736 would have required the alien to have performed at least 540 hours, or 90 work days, of agricultural work during a 12-month period. S. 1161 would have required at least 900 hours, or 150 work days, of agricultural work during a similar period. To qualify for adjustment to LPR status, S. 1313/H.R. 2736 would have required at least 540 hours, or 90 work days, of agricultural work in each of three years during a four-year period. S. 1161 would have required at least 900 hours, or 150 work days, of agricultural work in each of four years during a specified six-year period.

Various issues and concerns raised in connection with such earned adjustment proposals for agricultural workers may be relevant in assessing other guest worker legalization programs. Among these issues is the feasibility of program participants' meeting the applicable requirements to obtain legal status. S. 1161, for example, was criticized for incorporating work requirements for legalization that, some observers said, many agricultural workers could not satisfy. It also has been argued that multi-year work requirements could lead to exploitation, if workers were loathe to complain about work-related matters for fear of being fired before they had worked the requisite number of years. A possible countervailing set of considerations involves the continued availability of workers for low-skilled industries, such as agriculture, meat packing, and services industries. Some parties have expressed a general concern that a quick legalization process with light work requirements could soon deprive employers of needed workers, if some newly legalized workers were to leave certain industries to pursue more desirable job opportunities.

Treatment of Family Members

The treatment of family members under a guest worker proposal is likely to be an issue. Currently, the INA allows for the admission of the spouses and minor children of alien workers on H-2A, H-2B and other "H" visas who are accompanying the worker or following to join the worker in the United States. In considering any new program, one question would be whether guest workers coming from abroad could be accompanied by their spouses and children.

If the guest worker program in question were open to unauthorized aliens in the United States, the issue of family members would become much more complicated. Relevant questions would include the following: Would the unauthorized spouse and/or minor children of the prospective guest worker be granted some type of legal temporary resident status under the program? If not, would they be expected to leave, or be removed from, the country? If the program had a legalization component, would the spouse and children be eligible for LPR status as derivatives of the guest worker?

The treatment of family members became a significant issue in the 1986 legalization programs described above. As enacted, IRCA required all aliens to qualify for legalization on their own behalf; it made no provision for granting derivative LPR status to spouses and children. Legalized aliens, thus, needed to file immigrant visa petitions on behalf of their family members. These filings were primarily in the family preference category covering spouses and children of LPRs (category 2A) and had the effect of lengthening waiting times in this category.[48] To partially address the increased demand for visa numbers, the Immigration Act of 1990[49] made a limited number of additional visa numbers available for spouses and children of IRCA-legalized aliens for FY1992 through FY1994. It also provided for temporary stays of deportation and work authorization for certain spouses and children of IRCA-legalized aliens in the United States.

As suggested by the experience of the IRCA programs, the treatment of family members in any guest worker program with a legalization component could have broad implications for the U.S. immigration system. Even in the absence of a legalization component, however, the treatment of family members in a guest worker program could have important ramifications. With respect to the program itself, for example, it could affect the willingness of aliens to apply to participate.

Labor Market Test

A key question about any guest worker program is the type of labor market conditions that would have to exist, if any, in order for an employer to import alien workers.[50] Under both the H-2A and H-2B programs, employers interested in hiring foreign workers must first go through the process of labor certification. Intended to protect job opportunities for U.S. workers, labor certification entails a determination of whether qualified U.S. workers are available to perform the needed work and whether the hiring of foreign workers will adversely affect the wages and working conditions of similarly employed U.S. workers. As described above, recruitment is the primary method used to determine U.S. worker availability. While there is widespread agreement on the goals of labor certification, the process itself has been criticized for being cumbersome, slow, and ineffective in protecting U.S. workers.[51]

A proposed guest worker program could retain some form of labor certification or could establish a different process for determining if employers could bring in foreign workers. As described above, past legislative proposals to reform the H-2A program sought to overhaul current labor certification requirements by, for example, establishing a system of worker registries. Another option suggested by some in H-2A reform debates is to adopt the more streamlined labor market test used in the temporary worker program for professional specialty workers (H-1B program). That test, known as labor attestation, requires employers to attest to various conditions. Some argue that labor attestation is inadequate for unskilled jobs without educational requirements.[52] Assuming that protecting U.S. workers remained a policy priority, the labor market test incorporated in any guest worker program would need to be evaluated to determine whether it would likely serve this purpose.

Numerical Limits

Related to the issues of labor market tests and U.S. worker protections is the question of numerical limitations on a guest worker program. A numerical cap provides a means, separate from the labor market test, of limiting the number of foreign workers. Currently, as explained above, the H-2A program is not numerically limited, while the H-2B program is capped at 66,000 visas per year. Like the H-2B program, other capped temporary worker programs have fixed statutory numerical limits. By contrast, a guest worker program that was outlined by former Senator Phil Gramm during the 107th Congress, but never introduced as legislation, included a different type of numerical cap — one that would have varied annually based on regional unemployment rates. According to the program prospectus released by Senator Gramm:

> Except for seasonal work, the number of guest workers permitted to enroll would be adjusted annually in response to changes in U.S. economic conditions, specifically unemployment rates, on a region-by-region basis.

Numerical limitations also are relevant in the context of unauthorized immigration. Some view a temporary worker program as a way to begin reducing the size of the current unauthorized alien population and/or future inflows. In light of the estimated current size and annual growth rate of the unauthorized population, it could be argued that a guest worker program would need to be sizeable to have any significant impact. On the other hand, critics contend that a guest worker program, especially a large one, would be a counterproductive means of controlling unauthorized immigration. In their view, temporary worker programs serve to increase, not reduce, the size of the unauthorized population.

Enforcement

Another important consideration is how the terms of a guest worker program would be enforced. Relevant questions include what types of mechanisms would be used to ensure that employers complied with program requirements. With respect to the H-2A program, for example, the INA authorizes the Labor Secretary to —

> take such actions, including imposing appropriate penalties and seeking appropriate injunctive relief and specific performance of contractual

obligations, as may be necessary to assure employer compliance with terms and conditions of employment ...[53]

A related question is whether the enforcement system would be complaint-driven or whether the appropriate entity could take action in the absence of a specific complaint.

Another enforcement-related question is what type of mechanism, if any, would be used to ensure that guest workers departed the country at the end of their authorized period of stay. Historically, the removal of aliens who have overstayed their visas and thereby lapsed into unauthorized status, but have not committed crimes, has not been a priority of the U.S. immigration system. Some have suggested that a large scale guest worker program could help address the problem of visa overstaying and unauthorized immigration generally by severely limiting job opportunities for unauthorized aliens. Others doubt, however, that large numbers of unauthorized residents would voluntarily leave the country; as explained above, they argue instead that a new guest worker program would likely increase the size of the unauthorized alien population as many guest workers opted to overstay their visas.

Other ideas have been put forth to facilitate the departure of temporary workers at the end of their authorized period of stay. One suggestion is to involve the workers' home countries in the guest worker program. Another option is to create an incentive for foreign workers to leave the United States by, for example, withholding or otherwise setting aside a sum of money for each worker that would only become available once the worker returned home. In evaluating any such financially based incentive system, it may be useful to consider, among other questions, how much money would be available to a typical worker and whether such an amount would likely provide an adequate incentive to return home.

Homeland Security

A final consideration relates to border and homeland security, matters of heightened concern since the terrorist attacks of September 11, 2001. Supporters of new temporary worker programs argue that such programs would make the United States more secure. They cite security-related benefits of knowing the identities of currently unknown individuals in the country and of legalizing the inflow of alien workers and thereby freeing border personnel to concentrate on potential criminal and terrorist threats. Opponents reject the idea that guest worker programs improve homeland security and generally focus on the dangers of rewarding immigration law violators with temporary or permanent legal status. Security concerns may affect various aspects of a temporary worker program. Possible security-related provisions that may be considered as part of a new guest worker program include special screening of participants, monitoring while in the United States, and issuance of fraud-resistant documents.

CONCLUSION

The question of a new guest worker program is controversial. A key reason for this is the interrelationship between the recent discussion of guest worker programs and the issue of unauthorized immigration. The size of the current resident unauthorized alien population in the United States, along with continued unauthorized immigration and related deaths at the U.S.-Mexico border, are major factors cited in support of a new temporary worker program. At the same time, the importance of enforcing immigration law and not rewarding illegal aliens with any type of legalized status are primary reasons cited in opposition to such a program. It would seem that some bridging of this gap on the unauthorized alien question —perhaps in some of the areas analyzed above — would be a prerequisite to gaining broad support for a guest worker proposal.

REFERENCES

[1] For additional information on these historical programs, see U.S. Congress, Senate Committee on the Judiciary, *Temporary Worker Programs: Background and Issues*, committee print, 96th Cong., 2nd sess., Feb. 1980.

[2] Act of June 27, 1952, ch. 477, codified at 8 U.S.C.§1101 *et seq.* The INA is the basis of current immigration law.

[3] P.L. 99-603, Nov. 6, 1986.

[4] For an overview of the INA's nonimmigrant visa categories, see CRS Report RL31381, *U.S. Immigration Policy on Temporary Admissions*, by Ruth Ellen Wasem.

[5] The H-2B program is not limited to workers of a particular skill level and has been used to import a variety of workers, including entertainers and athletes.

[6] Prior to Mar. 1, 2003, the H-2A and H-2B programs were administered by ETA and the Immigration and Naturalization Service (INS) of the

Department of Justice. The Homeland Security Act of 2002 (P.L. 107-296, Nov. 25, 2002) abolished INS and transferred most of its functions to DHS as of Mar. 1.

[7] See 8 C.F.R. §214.2(h)(5)(iv)(A). According to *Immigration and Nationality Law Handbook, 2001-02 Edition*, however, "both DOL and INS take a very restrictive approach regarding the length of time for which a [H-2A or H-2B] petition can be approved." See Donna L. Lipinski, "The H-2s — A Class of Their Own," *Immigration and Nationality Law Handbook, 2001-02 Edition*, vol. 2, pp. 86-87.

[8] The prevailing wage rate is the average wage paid to similarly employed workers in the occupation in the area of intended employment. Additional information about prevailing wages is available at [http://www.ows.doleta.gov/foreign/wages.asp].

[9] The AEWR is an hourly wage rate set by DOL for each state or region, based upon data gathered by the Department of Agriculture in quarterly wage surveys. For 2004, the AEWR ranges from $7.38 for Arkansas, Louisiana, and Mississippi to $9.60 for Hawaii. See CRS Report RL32861, *Farm Labor: The Adverse Effect Wage Rate (AEWR)*, by William G. Whittaker.

[10] Required wages and benefits under the H-2A program are set forth in 20 C.F.R. §655.102.

[11] H-2A workers, like nonimmigrants generally, are not eligible for federally funded public assistance, with the exception of Medicaid emergency services. For further information on alien eligibility for federal benefits, see CRS Report RL31114, *Noncitizen Eligibility for Major Federal Public Assistance Programs: Policies and Legislation*, by Ruth Ellen Wasem; and CRS Report RL31630, *Federal Funding for Unauthorized Aliens' Emergency Medical Expenses*, by Alison M. Siskin.

[12] See 8 C.F.R. §214.2(h)(9)(iii)(B).

[13] Included in this three-year period is any time an H-2B alien spent in the United States under the "H" (temporary worker) or "L" (temporary intracompany transferee) visa categories.

[14] While not subject to the broader transportation requirements of the H-2A program, H-2B employers are required by law to pay the reasonable costs of return transportation abroad for an H-2B worker who is dismissed prior to the end of his or her authorized period of stay.

[15] The proposed USCIS rule is available at [http://a257.g.akamaitech.net/7/257/2422/01jan20051800/edocket.access.gpo.gov/2005/05-1240.htm]. DOL has published a companion proposal,

which is available at [http://a257.g.akamaitech.net/7/257/2422/01jan20051800/edocket.access.gpo.gov/2005/05-1222.htm].

[16] For information on the H-1B nonimmigrant classification, see CRS Report RL30498, *Immigration: Legislative Issues on Nonimmigrant Professional Specialty (H-1B) Workers*, by Ruth Ellen Wasem.

[17] For definitions of these types of need, see 8 C.F.R. §214.2(h)(6)(ii).

[18] See INA §214(g)(1)(B).

[19] U.S. Department of Homeland Security, U.S. Citizenship and Immigration Services, "USCIS Reaches H-2B Cap," press release, Jan. 4, 2005.

[20] U.S. Department of Homeland Security, U.S. Citizenship and Immigration Services, "USCIS to Accept Additional H-2B Filings for FY2005 and FY2006," public notice, May 23, 2005.

[21] Jeffrey S. Passel, Randy Capps, and Michael Fix, *Undocumented Immigrants: Facts and Figures*, Urban Institute, Jan. 12, 2004; Jeffrey S. Passel, *Estimates of the Size and Characteristics of the Undocumented Population*, Pew Hispanic Center, Mar. 21, 2005; Jeffrey S. Passel, *The Size and Characteristics of the Unauthorized Migrant Population in the U.S.; Estimates Based on the March 2005 Current Population Survey*, Pew Hispanic Center, Mar. 7, 2006 (hereafter cited as Passel, *The Size and Characteristics of the Unauthorized Migrant Population in the U.S.*, Mar. 7, 2006). The latter two reports are available at [http://pewhispanic.org/topics/index.php?TopicID=16]. Also see CRS Report RS21938, *Unauthorized Aliens in the United States: Estimates Since 1986*, by Ruth Ellen Wasem.

[22] U.S. Department of Justice, Immigration and Naturalization Service, Office of Policy and Planning, *Estimates of the Unauthorized Immigrant Population Residing in the United States: 1990 to 2000*, Jan. 2003. Note: Other estimates of the unauthorized alien population in Jan. 2000 are higher. These disparities are accounted for, in part, by INS's narrower definition of an unauthorized alien.

[23] For further information on migrant deaths, see CRS Report RL32562, *Border Security: The Role of the U.S. Border Patrol*, by Blas Nuñez-Neto.

[24] Passel, *The Size and Characteristics of the Unauthorized Migrant Population in the U.S.*, Mar. 7, 2006, at [http://pewhispanic.org/reports/report.php?ReportID=61].

[25] Ibid., pp. 10-11.

[26] Philip Martin, *Guest Workers: New Solution, New Problem?*, Pew Hispanic Center Study, Mar. 21, 2002.

[27] For additional information about these legislative proposals, see CRS Report RL30852, *Immigration of Agricultural Guest Workers: Policy, Trends, and Legislative Issues*, by Ruth Ellen Wasem and Geoffrey K. Collver. (Hereafter cited as CRS Report RL30852.)

[28] During the 107th Congress, former Senator Phil Gramm released a preliminary proposal for a new U.S.-Mexico guest worker program that would have covered both agricultural and nonagricultural workers, but he did not introduce legislation.

[29] Although S. 1814 and H.R. 4056 are not identical, they are treated as companion bills for the purposes of this discussion because they are highly similar.

[30] For a discussion of the U.S. system of permanent admissions, including numerical limits, see CRS Report RL32235, *U.S. Immigration Policy on Permanent Admissions*, by Ruth Ellen Wasem. (Hereafter cited as CRS Report RL32235.)

[31] For information on noncitizen eligibility for federal public benefits, see CRS Report RL31114, *Noncitizen Eligibility for Major Federal Public Assistance Programs: Policies and Legislation*, by Ruth Ellen Wasem.

[32] This description of S. 1837 is based on both the bill text and clarifications provided by Sen. Cornyn's office by telephone on July 22, 2003. Some clarifying language may need to be added to the bill.

[33] Although S. 352 and H.R. 793 are not identical, they are treated as companion bills here because they are nearly identical and none of their differences are substantive. The full short title of S. 352 is Save Our Small and Seasonal Businesses of 2005.

[34] Note: The blue card status proposed under this bill is different than the blue card status proposed in S. 2087 (discussed in a separate section below).

[35] For information on numerical limits, see CRS Report RL32235.

[36] For a discussion of visa priority dates, see CRS Report RL32235.

[37] For information on numerical limits, see CRS Report RL32235.

[38] For information on the entry-exit system issue, see CRS Report RL32234, *U.S. Visitor and Immigrant Status Indicator Technology (US-VISIT) Program*, by Lisa M. Seghetti and Stephen R. Viña.

[39] For an explanation of INA §245(i), see CRS Report RL31373, *Immigration: Adjustment to Permanent Resident Status Under Section 245(i)*, by Andorra Bruno.

[40] INA §212(a)(9)(B). This ground of inadmissibility, known as the "3 and 10 year bars," applies to aliens who have been unlawfully present in the United States for more than 180 days and who then depart or are removed.

[41] The Administration did *not* offer a detailed legislative proposal. Some materials on the Administration proposal, however, are available on the White House website. The President's Jan. 7, 2004, remarks on the proposal are available at [http://www.whitehouse.gov/news/releases/2004/01/print/20040107-3.html]. A fact sheet on the proposal, entitled *Fair and Secure Immigration Reform* is available at [http://www.whitehouse.gov/news/releases/2004/01/print/20040107-3.html]. The transcript of a Jan. 6, 2004 background briefing for reporters is available at [http://www.whitehouse.gov/news/releases/2004/01/print/20040106-3.html].

[42] Secretary Chao's written testimony is available at [http://judiciary.senate.gov/hearing .cfm?id=1634].

[43] Comment of T. Alexander Aleinikoff, Migration Policy Institute. Quoted in Eric Schmitt, "The Nation: Separate and Unequal; You Can Come In. You Stay Out," *New York Times*, July 29, 2001, Section 4, p. 5.

[44] President Bush was asked in July 2001 whether an immigration proposal under consideration at the time to legalize the status of some unauthorized Mexicans would be expanded to cover immigrants from other countries. The President responded, "We'll consider all folks here," but did not provide further details. See Edwin Chen and Jonathan Peterson, "Bush Hints at Broader Amnesty," *Los Angeles Times*, July 27, 2001, Part A, part 1, p. 1.

[45] For example, in an Aug. 2001 letter to President Bush and Mexican President Vicente Fox setting forth the Democrats' immigration principles, then-Senate Majority Leader Thomas Daschle and then-House Minority Leader Richard Gephardt stated that "no migration proposal can be complete without an earned adjustment program."

[46] P.L. 99-603, Nov. 6, 1986. The general legalization program is at INA §245A, and the SAW program is at INA §210.

[47] Certain individuals who had not legalized under the general program and were participants in specified class action lawsuits were given a new time-limited opportunity to adjust to LPR status by the Legal Immigration Family Equity Act (LIFE; P.L. 106-553, Appendix B, Title XI, Dec. 21, 2000) and the LIFE Act Amendments (P.L. 106-554, Appendix D, Title XV, Dec. 21, 2000).

[48] See CRS Report RL32235.

[49] P.L. 101-649, Nov. 29, 1990.

[50] Questions about the existence of industry-wide labor shortages are outside the scope of this report. For a discussion of the shortage issue with respect to agriculture, see CRS Report RL30395, *Farm Labor Shortages and*

Immigration Policy, by Linda Levine. Also see CRS Report 95-712, *The Effects on U.S. Farm Workers of an Agricultural Guest Worker Program*, by Linda Levine.

[51] See U.S. Department of Labor, Office of Inspector General, *Consolidation of Labor's Enforcement Responsibilities for the H-2A Program Could Better Protect U.S. Agricultural Workers*, Report Number 04-98-004-03-321, Mar. 31, 1998.

[52] See CRS Report RL30852.

[53] INA §218(g)(2).

INDEX

D

E

F

G

H

I

S

T

U

V

W